PROJECT KID

AMANDA KINGLOFF

PHOTOGRAPHS BY
ALEXANDRA GRABLEWSKI

ARTISAN
NEW YORK

Published by Artisan
A division of Workman Publishing Company, Inc.
225 Varick Street
New York, NY 10014-4381
artisanbooks.com

Published simultaneously in Canada by Thomas Allen & Son, Limited

Library of Congress Cataloging-in-Publication Data
Kingloff, Amanda.
Project Kid : 100 ingenious crafts for family fun / Amanda Kingloff.
   pages   cm
Includes index.
ISBN 978-1-57965-514-3
1. Handicraft. 2. Children's paraphernalia. I. Title. II. Title: Project Kid.
TT157.K437   2014
745.5—dc23   2013029988

Design by Michelle Ishay-Cohen

Printed in China
First printing, March 2014

10 9 8 7 6 5 4 3 2 1

For my muses,
Oliver and Sommer

CONTENTS

5
READY TO WEAR

6
THE GREAT OUTDOORS

7
ABSTRACT EXPRESSIONS

PLUS!
ART LESSONS
**YARN POM-POMS (56), WEAVING (86),
FRINGING (120), MOSAIC (168),
FABRIC DYEING (210), HOMEMADE CLAY (242)**

Introduction

A single moment with my son inspired this entire book. As I was returning gift-wrap supplies to my craft room one day, Oliver (then two years old) pointed at my spool of ribbon and said, "Hey Mommy, a balloon!" I stopped and looked down at what was in my hands—a cardboard circle with a trail of thin, yellow grosgrain ribbon hanging down to the floor. To him, a circle with a line dropping downward was a balloon—no matter that it wasn't made of latex or floating in the air. I realized he was onto something.

The projects in this book organically took shape once I began looking at the world through my son's eyes, going back to that time when everything was just shapes and colors and the purpose of objects had no meaning to me. Combing the grocery aisles was no longer about shopping for oatmeal and crackers, it was about finding materials to make bongo drums or a miniature village. Cotton balls were no longer just for removing nail polish—they became a sheep's curly wool, stuffed a doll's pillow, and morphed into cotton candy.

It's the mixture of the repurposed materials with common craft supplies that brings the projects in these chapters to life. With over 100 crafts that teach kids basic techniques and the joy that comes from invention, there is something special and surprising here for toddlers, teens, and every age in between.

So start saving your bottle caps and cardboard tubes. Build a treasure chest of found objects. Who knows? Maybe your young crafter will turn that scrap of ribbon into a necklace, a fishing pole, or even the string of a paper plate balloon.

Getting Started

Before you get crafting, you'll need a handful of basic materials and tools. But you don't need to rush to the store to buy an identical version of every supply that you see pictured in this book. I'm a craft designer, and your kids are too! Play with what you have, and occasionally splurge on something a project just can't do without. If you're willing, let your kids raid your button collection (you don't still have that pink blouse, do you?), your gift-wrap scraps, and the stash of knitting yarn that you swear you'll one day make into a scarf.

You will see that on nearly every page of this book, there is at least one supply that you already have, that you probably never thought of as a craft material, or that might otherwise be headed for the trash or recycling bin. And if you're stumped as to whether to keep or toss something, just ask the expert—your kid.

A note on safety: Crafting with little ones should always go hand in hand with adult supervision and assistance, so please pay attention to the tools required. I recommend all hot-glue-gun use, wire clipping, and some of the more difficult cardboard cutting be assisted by an adult. Know your child's capabilities, but put safety first. If you have children under the age of four working near or alongside you, be aware of materials that could be choking hazards like beads, buttons, and other small objects.

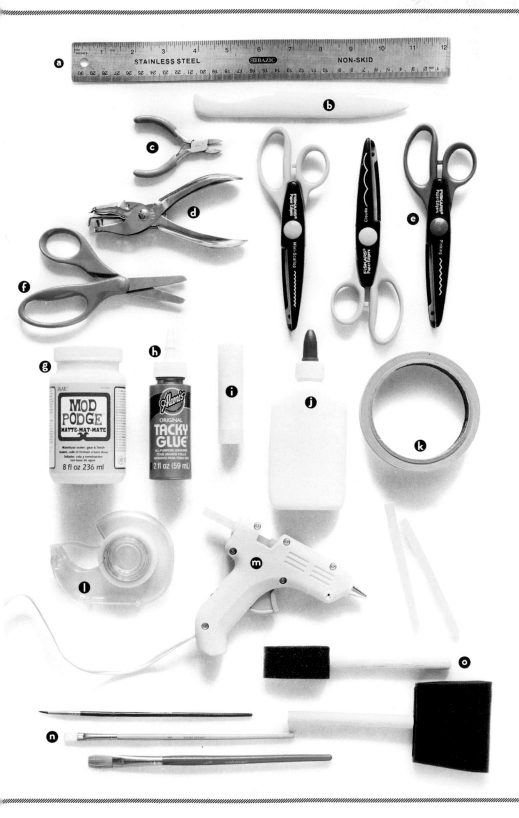

ESSENTIAL TOOLS

a. **Ruler**

b. **Bone folder**

c. **Wire clippers**
   Best if used by an adult, because some wire requires a little muscle to cut through.

d. **Hole punch**

e. **Decorative-edge scissors**

f. **Scissors**

g. **Mod Podge**
   Or make your own by mixing one part craft glue with one part water.

h. **Tacky glue**

i. **Glue stick**

j. **White craft glue**

k. **Masking tape**

l. **Clear tape**

m. **Hot-glue gun**
   This is an adults-only tool and should be used away from kids and pets.

n. **Paintbrushes**

o. **Foam brushes**

CRAFTY MATERIALS

a. Dimensional paint
b. Tempera paint
c. Acrylic paint
d. Craft wood sticks
e. Pom-poms
   Learn how to make your own on page 57.
f. Craft foam
g. Scrapbooking paper
h. Tissue paper
i. Notebook paper
j. Crepe paper
k. Pipe cleaners
l. Glitter
m. Colored pencils
n. Permanent marker
   You may want to closely supervise the use of these.
o. Paint pens
p. Markers
q. Crayons
r. Felt
s. Ink pads
t. Ribbon
u. String
v. Decorative tape
w. Beads
x. Embroidery hoops
y. Buttons
z. Yarn

HOUSEHOLD ITEMS

a. Kraft paper
b. Wax paper
c. Newspaper
d. Clothespins
e. Toothpicks
f. Jar lids
g. Magazines
h. Plastic bottles
i. Glass bottles
j. Bottle caps
k. Jars
l. Cardboard food and juice boxes
m. Cardboard
n. Paper towel tubes
o. Toilet paper tubes
p. Cotton balls
q. Cotton swabs

ANIMAL KINGDOM

Projects that bark,
hoot, and baa!

BIRDY BOTTLE BOOKEND

Wondering what to do with orphaned socks? A lone baby sock makes a perfect penguin head!

WHAT YOU'LL NEED

- One 17-ounce plastic drink bottle
- 2 to 3 cups of sand
- Funnel
- 1 baby sock
- 4 to 5 cotton balls
- White and yellow felt
- Scissors
- 2 tiny black pom-poms (available at Michaels Stores)
- Tacky glue
- One 2½-inch piece of wire
- One 2 cm felt bead (available from TadaaStudio.com)
- 1 Tyvek envelope
- Washi tape (available from HappyTape.com)
- 2 colors of yarn

1 Clean out the bottle and remove all labels. Fill it with sand and replace the cap.

2 To make the penguin's head, stuff the baby sock with cotton balls and slip it over the top of the bottle.

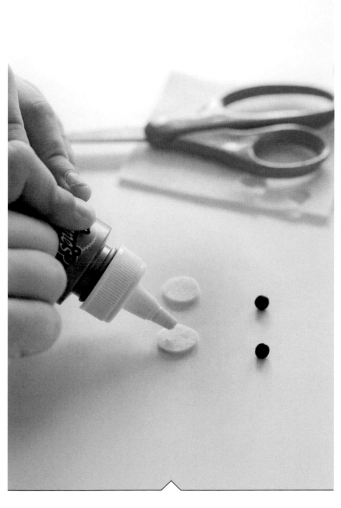

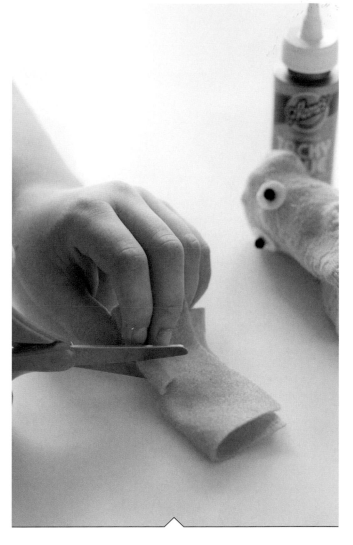

3 To make the eyes, cut two circles about the size of a plain M&M from white felt. Glue a tiny black pom-pom to each. Glue the circles onto the sock.

4 To make the beak, fold a piece of yellow felt and cut a ¼-inch triangle on the crease. Glue the crease onto the sock about ½ inch below the eyes.

5 To make the earmuffs, bend the wire into a headband shape. Cut the felt bead in half and glue a piece to each end of the wire, rounded side facing out. Slip the earmuffs onto the penguin's head and glue to secure.

6 Cut two wing shapes (pointed at one end, cut straight across on the other) from the Tyvek envelope, about two-thirds the height of your bottle and about 3 inches across at the widest point. Cover the wings with strips of washi tape and glue the top, straight edge of each wing around the neck of the bottle.

7 To give the penguin a scarf, braid three 20-inch strands of yarn (the finished scarf will be about 16 inches long). If the yarn is thin, you may want to double or triple it (as shown) to give it some thickness.

8 Finally, to make the feet, fold a 3-inch square of yellow felt in half and cut a 2-inch-tall half heart shape on the crease. Glue it to the bottom of the bottle, rounded points facing out.

COTTON-BALL SHEEP

Have a family craft night and make a sheep for every member of your brood.

WHAT YOU'LL NEED

- **2 plastic eggs, 1 large and 1 small**
- **Cotton balls (about 50)**
- **Tacky glue**
- **4 lollipop sticks (available at Michaels Stores)**
- **Black permanent marker**
- **Hot-glue gun**
- **Black washi tape (available from HappyTape.com)**
- **1 cotton swab**
- **Two ⅜-inch white shank buttons (buttons with a loop on the back)**

1 To make the body, affix cotton balls all over the large plastic egg with tacky glue. Let it dry.

2 To make the legs, color the lollipop sticks with black marker. Holding the egg horizontally, hot-glue two sticks toward the front of the egg and two toward the back in a V formation. While the glue is still wet, twist the sticks one turn to firmly plant them into the cotton balls.

3 To make the head, cover the small egg with torn pieces of washi tape. Add glue to the tape pieces to keep them adhered, when needed.

4 To make the ears, cut the cotton swab in half and wrap the soft ends in washi tape. Glue the cut ends of the swabs to the point of the small egg, and glue two cotton balls on top. Hot-glue the head to the body.

5 To make the eyes, color black dots on the buttons and hot-glue to the head.

JOINER-BISCUIT BUTTERFLIES

No insects were harmed
in the making of this craft.

WHAT YOU'LL NEED

- 12 joiner biscuits, six size 10 and six size 20 (available at Lowe's)

- Dimensional paint in three or four different colors

- 3 wooden demitasse spoons (available from ShopSweetLulu.com)

- Scissors

- Hot-glue gun

- Black twine

- One 7-by-15½-inch shadow box frame (available at Michaels Stores)

- 6 ball head straight pins (optional)

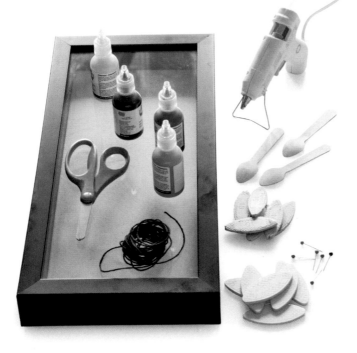

Biscuits are intended to be used to join two pieces of wood together after they've been cut with a tool called a biscuit joiner. But they look a lot prettier as butterfly wings.

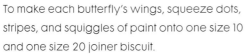
To make each butterfly's wings, squeeze dots, stripes, and squiggles of paint onto one size 10 and one size 20 joiner biscuit.

Press blank matching-sized biscuits on top of the painted ones, and then pull each set apart to produce mirror painted surfaces on the second biscuits. Let them dry, about 3 hours.

3 Cut off about 1 inch from the spoon handles. Hot-glue the bottom points of the biscuits to the front of each spoon handle, with two longer ones on top and two smaller ones on the bottom.

4 To create the antennae, cut 1- to 2-inch pieces of black twine, fold them in half, and glue the crease to the back of each butterfly head. Mount the butterflies in the shadow box frame either with ball head straight pins or by hot-gluing them to the frame backing.

JUICE-BOX OWL

Juice boxes can be made into any vehicle or building block—or in this case, the body of an adorable owl.

WHAT YOU'LL NEED

- 1 juice box, emptied and cleaned
- One 12-by-12-inch piece of patterned craft paper
- Clear tape
- Wool felt (available from MagicCabin.com)
- Scissors
- Pumpkin seeds (about 50)
- Tacky glue
- 2 cotton balls
- 1 basket coffee filter
- Yellow watercolor paint
- Paintbrush
- 2 wooden beads

1 Wrap the juice box in the patterned craft paper like you would a present. Tape to seal.

2 Cut two wing shapes from the felt. Each wing should be as tall as the box, with the top, straight edge ½ inch wider than the side of the box, and the center of the wing 3 inches wide.

3

To create a feather pattern, glue pumpkin seeds on the wings and let the glue set. Depending on the height of your box, you'll need about sixteen seeds per wing.

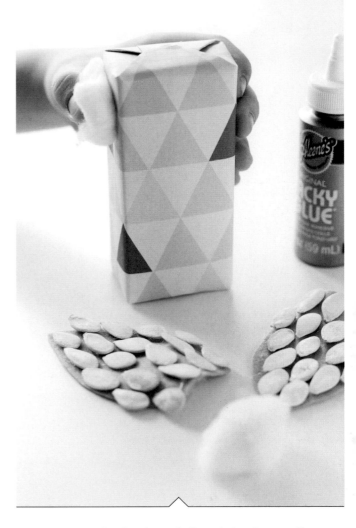

4

To give shape to the wings, glue a cotton ball on both top side edges of the box, and glue the wings on top of them.

6 Cut a 1-inch-wide ring from the ruffled edge of the coffee filter and then cut it in half. Bunch up the strip to create a rosette shape, twist the back half into a short stem, and wrap tape around the back to secure. Repeat with the other half of the ring.

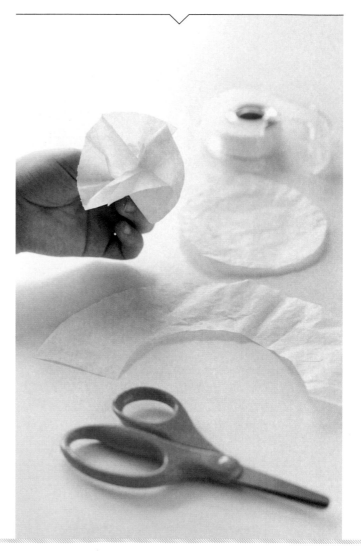

5. To create the eyes, paint the coffee filter with the watercolor paint. Just give it a light, washy coat and let it dry.

7

To create the eyes, glue five or six pumpkin seeds in a circle on each filter rosette, and then glue a bead in the center. Glue the rosettes side by side to the top of the box.

8

Glue a pumpkin seed in between the rosettes as the nose, and two on the bottom of the wrapped juice box as the feet.

PAINTED-FEATHER PEACOCK FAN

Mother Nature really got it right with peacock feathers. Stick with her color scheme or shake it up.

WHAT YOU'LL NEED

- 8 to 10 white feathers
- Acrylic paint in blue, yellow, green, and turquoise
- Paintbrushes
- Gold glitter glue
- Blue and yellow craft paper
- Pencil
- Scissors
- Tacky glue

1 Paint the feathers as shown or in your own design. Let dry.

2 Add glitter glue embellishments—tiny dots or thin stripes are best. Let dry.

3 To create the peacock's body, draw a 2-inch tall figure eight on the back of the blue craft paper; make the top oval about half the size of the bottom one. Cut along the outside edge of the figure eight, leaving about ⅛ inch of space around it.

4 For the beak, cut a tiny triangle from the yellow craft paper and glue it, pointing down, to the small end of the figure eight.

5 To create your fan, cut a 1-inch square from either color of craft paper and glue the bottom points of your feathers to it close together in a fan shape.

6 Finish by gluing the large side of the figure eight on top of the junction of the feathers.

When you paint the feathers, lay them out on a paper towel. Paint the first color on all of them, then the second, and so on, so you don't have to keep washing your brush in between feathers.

WILDLIFE PRESERVED

Even vegetarians can't protest the awesomeness of these decoupaged animal masks.

WHAT YOU'LL NEED

- Magazines, catalogs, newspapers
- Scissors
- Rabbit, cat, and zebra masks (available from CostumeCraze.com)
- Mod Podge
- 1-inch foam brush
- Cardboard
- White paint
- Paintbrush
- Twine
- Hot-glue gun
- Six 3 cm black felt beads (available from TadaaStudio.com)

FOR THE RABBIT
- Hole punch
- 1 colored brad
- Stiff thread

FOR THE CAT
- Tacky glue
- Stiff thread

FOR THE ZEBRA
- One 2-inch book ring

1 Cut like-colored shapes, about 2 inches square, from magazines, newspapers, and catalogs. (Stripes like the zebra's will require two different colors.) Using a foam brush, coat each mask with a thin layer of Mod Podge; lay your paper on top of it, then cover the paper with another layer of Mod Podge. Press the paper in and around the contours of the masks. Cut cardboard to mimic the shapes of trophy mounting panels, paint them white, and let them dry. Hot-glue twine to the backs for hanging.

2 *For the rabbit:* To make the flower, cut four 1-inch-wide vertical strips from a magazine. Punch a hole at either end of each strip, and one in the middle. Insert the brad into the center of all of the strips, then make loops by slipping the holes at the ends of the strips over the brad. Fold back the arms of the brad and hot-glue it to the base of the rabbit's ear. To make the rabbit's whiskers, cut six 3-inch-long pieces of thread and glue to the rabbit's nose. Glue a felt bead into each eye socket.

3 *For the cat*: To make the bow tie, accordion fold a black magazine page. The folds should be ½ to ¾ inch wide. Cut a small piece from another magazine page, about ½ inch by 1 inch. Gather the folded paper together in the middle and glue the small piece around it. Glue the bow tie under the cat's chin. To make the cat's whiskers, cut six 3-inch-long pieces of thread and glue three to either side of the cat's nose. Glue a felt bead into each eye socket.

4 *For the zebra*: To make the earring, Mod Podge pieces of gold-colored magazine paper around the open book ring. Let the paper dry and then squeeze the ring closed around the zebra's ear. You can use a hole punch to "pierce" his ear, but, depending on the shape of your mask's ear, it may not be necessary. Glue a felt bead into each eye socket.

YARN BIRDCAGE

Craft a bird or just cut one out of paper for this whimsical cage made out of yarn.

WHAT YOU'LL NEED

- 1 balloon
- 1 cylindrical vase (approximately 5 by 5 inches)
- Painter's tape
- Plastic wrap
- Cookie sheet lined with wax paper
- Yellow yarn
- Scissors
- Aleene's Fabric Stiffener & Draping Liquid (available at Michaels Stores)
- Disposable cup
- 1 large bead
- Hot-glue gun
- One 2- to 3-inch-long dowel or stick
- Two 7-inch pieces of cord
- Twine

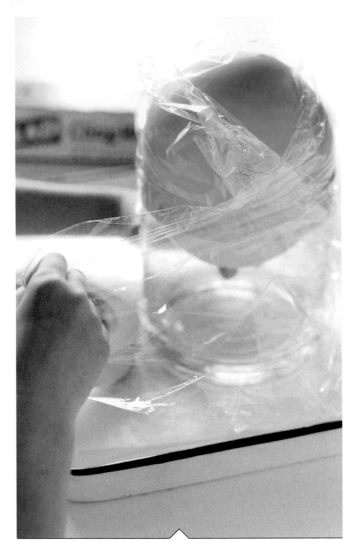

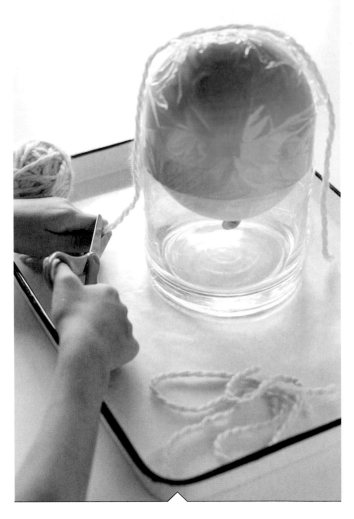

1 Blow up the balloon until it fits snugly in the vase. Adhere a piece of painter's tape around where the balloon meets the edge of the vase, securing the balloon in place, then cover the whole thing in plastic wrap. Place on the cookie sheet.

2 Cut eight pieces of yarn that are long enough to extend from the bottom edge of the vase, over the balloon, to the bottom edge of the vase on the other side.

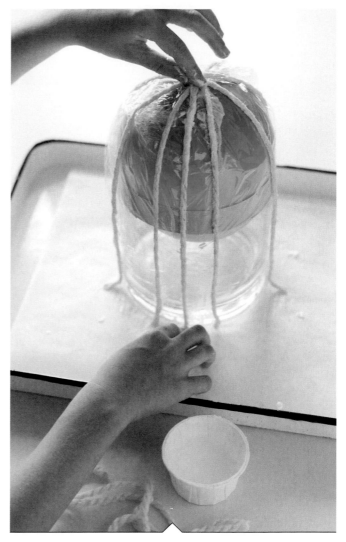

3 Pour fabric stiffener into the disposable cup. Dip one piece of yarn into the fabric stiffener and squeeze off the excess. Drape the yarn over the top of the balloon, centered (let any excess rest on the wax paper). Smooth the yarn down over the surface of the balloon and vase. Repeat, adhering the next piece exactly perpendicular to the first. Repeat two more times, forming an asterisk shape.

4 Cut the remaining four pieces of yarn in half. One by one, dip these pieces in fabric stiffener and adhere between two of the bars created in step 3.

5 Cut three pieces of yarn to wrap around the circumference of the vase, dip one into the fabric stiffener, and wrap around the balloon where it meets the vase. Repeat with a second piece of yarn, ½ inch below the first. Wrap the third piece around the base of the vase.

6 To make the hanger ring, cut a 4-inch piece of yarn, dip it into the fabric stiffener, and form a flat circle on the wax paper. Set the cookie sheet aside and let the yarn dry, about 4 hours.

7 Once the yarn is hard and dry to the touch, use scissors to pop the balloon. Wiggle the cage off of the vase, plastic wrap, and balloon. With your fingers, scrape off the excess dried fabric stiffener. Trim off excess yarn on the bottom of the cage.

8 Hot-glue the bead to the top of the cage, then glue the dried yarn circle on top of that. To make the bird's perch, tie the dowel to two pieces of cord, thread the cords through the holes in the cage, and knot behind the hanger. Thread the twine through the top loop for hanging.

POM-POM POODLE PULL TOY

Doggone it! Every baby should have a homemade pull toy.

WHAT YOU'LL NEED

- Cardboard

- Pen or pencil

- Scissors

- 12 small red, 4 large red, and 5 small pink yarn pom-poms (available from eeBoo.com, or make your own—see page 57)

- Tacky glue

- 1 pipe cleaner

- White felt

- 3 tiny black pom-poms

- 3 Matchbox cars

- 2 tongue depressors

- Yarn

 Draw a 4-inch-tall-by-5-inch-long dog on cardboard and cut it out. Don't worry if your dog isn't perfect or poodlelike—a general canine shape will work.

Glue red yarn pom-poms to one side of the dog—two small ones on each leg, two large ones on the body, and two more small ones for the head and snout. Glue two pink pom-poms on top of the bottommost pom-poms to make the paws. Repeat on the other side of the cardboard dog.

3 To make the dog's tail, cut a 3-inch length of pipe cleaner and glue a pink pom-pom to the end. Poke the other end into the cardboard and secure it with glue.

4 To make the ears, cut two small teardrop shapes, about 1 inch tall, from the felt. Glue the pointed ends to the sides of the dog's head and finish the dog's face by gluing the tiny black pom-poms onto the head and snout as the eyes and nose.

5 To make the base of the pull toy, glue a 12-by-4-inch piece of felt around a 6-by-4-inch piece of cardboard.

6 Glue the Matchbox cars to the underside of the cardboard (one in front, two in back).

7 Glue a tongue depressor to each side of the base to cover the cardboard edges.

8 To make the pull cord, braid six 30-inch-long strands of yarn together to make a 24-inch cord. Glue it to the underside of the base, in front of the single car. Glue the dog's feet to the top of the base.

NEEDLEPOINT FLYSWATTER

You'll definitely hear "Ooh!" not "Ew!"
when your friends see these
hanging on the wall.

WHAT YOU'LL NEED

- **Yarn in various colors**
- **Kid-safe needle**
- **Scissors**
- **Mesh flyswatter**

Follow the stitch guides on the following pages to create the bug of your choice.

1 To begin, cut a long piece of yarn, about 24 inches, and tie a couple of knots at one end.

2 Thread a needle through the opposite end of the yarn.

3 Begin stitching by inserting the needle through the underside of the flyswatter, pulling until the knot catches. Following your guide, pull the yarn across the correct number of squares, inserting the needle back into the flyswatter when you reach the end of a line.

4 Repeat until you've finished stitching a color, then knot the yarn on the underside of the flyswatter and trim off the excess. Repeat with the remaining colors.

FLYSWATTER STITCH GUIDES

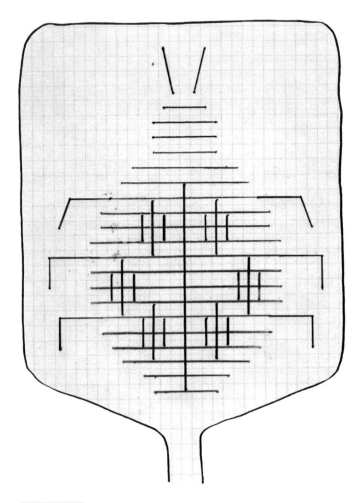

LADYBUG

Start with the red body and then stitch the black legs, carrying the yarn across the underside of the body to do the leg on the opposite side. When moving to the next set of legs, thread the yarn under the red stitches on the underside of the flyswatter. Finish the legs, then stitch the head and antennae. Tie off the black yarn and cut a new piece. Stitch a center line and six ladybug spots (made with three parallel lines), three on either side of the line.

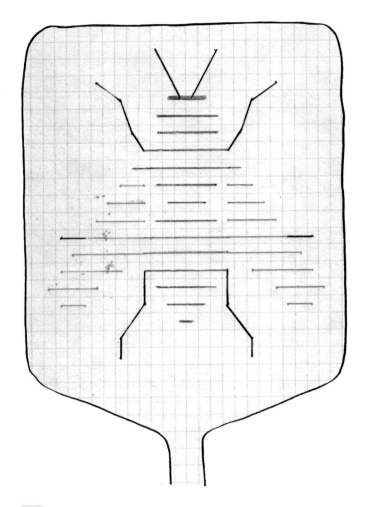

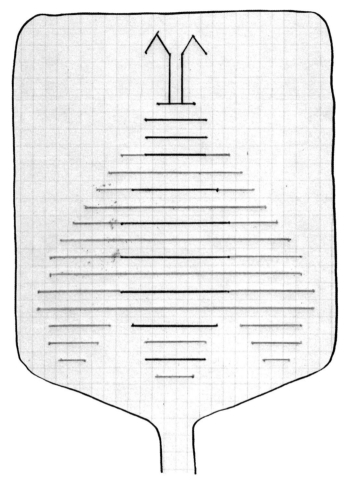

FLY

Begin with the gray body, then do the blue wings, starting both toward the head of the bug. When beginning with the black yarn, start with the antennae. Before stitching the top two legs, thread your needle under the stitches on the underside of the fly's head so that you do not see the black yarn through the mesh. Do this again under its lower body when you reach the bottom two legs.

BUMBLEBEE

Start with the black antennae and continue down to the head and stripes to complete all the black stitching. Start the yellow stitching at the top near the head and work your way down the wings and body.

ART LESSON:
YARN POM-POMS

Turn the page for four projects that use pom-poms!

Fiber arts have been around for centuries, but very often kids are left out of the fun—either because children wielding needles of any sort need close supervision or because fiber arts are thought to be too complicated for little hands.

But they don't have to be complicated. Instead of jumping into a fancy knitting project or a king-sized quilt, start off with simple, basic crafts. The pom-pom is a perfect place to begin because all you need is yarn and scissors—and so many cute things can be made from it. Start with a thick yarn; you'll need less of it to make a full, satisfying pom-pom.

WHAT YOU'LL NEED

- Yarn
- A fork, a smartphone, cardboard, a deck of cards, or a small book (optional)
- Scissors

1 To choose what base to wrap your yarn around, first decide what size you'd like your pom-pom to be. A fork is great for a 1-inch pom-pom, and a smartphone works well for a 2- to 3-inch version. You can also use your fingers, a piece of cardboard, a deck of cards, or a small book.

2 Wrap yarn around your chosen form fifty to eighty times until it becomes a thick bundle. Cut the bundle free from the ball of yarn and slip it off the form. If you're using a fork, you can actually tie off the bundle by wrapping the yarn through the middle tines before slipping it off the fork.

3 Otherwise, to tie off your bundle, cut a piece of yarn, about 4 inches for a small pom-pom and 6 to 8 inches for a larger one, and tie it very tightly around the center of the slipped-off bundle.

4 Insert your scissors into the loops of your yarn bundle and snip until each loop is cut.

5 Fluff your pom-pom and trim so that all sides are even.

POM-POM PROJECTS

2

FUZZY KEY CHAIN

WHAT YOU'LL NEED

- Three 8-inch pieces of leather cord
- Yarn
- Fork (optional)
- Scissors
- 9 wooden beads
- 1 key ring

1 Make a knot at the bottom of one piece of leather cord.

2 Begin making a 1-inch pom-pom as instructed in steps 1 and 2 on page 57, but before you tie off the yarn bundle, lay the leather cord parallel to the bundle.

3 Now knot your small piece of yarn around the bundle and the leather cord as tightly as you can. Pull the cord until the knot meets the center tie, then finish the pom-pom normally.

4 String three beads onto the cord and tie a knot to keep them in place.

5 Make two more pom-pom cords, knot all three together, then braid. Tie them to the key ring.

1

CUTE CHICK

WHAT YOU'LL NEED

- Orange felt
- Scissors
- Glue
- One 1-inch pom-pom
- Pliers
- 2 bobby pins
- One 2-inch pom-pom

1 To create a beak, fold a piece of orange felt and cut a ½-inch triangle on the fold. Glue the beak to the 1-inch pom-pom to make the head.

2 Take pliers and bend each bobby pin about ½ inch from the open end. (You'll need a little adult muscle for this.)

3 Glue the 1-inch pom-pom to the 2-inch pom-pom, and then glue the bobby pins to the bottom of the larger pom-pom, ½ to ¾ inch apart, as the feet.

3

PENCIL BLOOM

WHAT YOU'LL NEED

- 1 pencil cap eraser
- Scissors
- Glue
- One 1-inch pom-pom
- Dark and light green felt
- 1 pencil

1 Cut about ½ inch off of the point of the pencil cap eraser and glue the pom-pom to the remaining cap. Place on the end of the pencil.

2 Cut 1-inch leaves out of light green felt. Cut two skinny ¾-inch ovals out of dark green felt, cut these in half, and hot-glue them on top of the light green leaves.

3 Hot-glue the leaves to the sides of the pencil. (They pull off easily when it's time to move them to a new pencil.)

4

FAUX FRUIT

WHAT YOU'LL NEED

- Scissors
- One 3-inch yellow pom-pom
- One 4-inch red pom-pom
- Glue
- Two 1-inch twigs
- Green felt
- Ten to twelve 1-inch purple pom-poms, with untrimmed 8-inch strings tying off the center of the bundles

1 *For the lemon:* Trim the yellow pom-pom into the shape of a lemon.

2 *For the apple:* Cut a small indentation at the top of the red pom-pom and glue a 1-inch twig into the indentation. Cut a ¾- to 1-inch leaf from green felt and glue it to the stem.

3 *For the grapes:* For each purple pom-pom, trim one side of the 8-inch strings to the length of the pom-pom and leave one long. Tie the strings together to make a bunch of grapes, tying the top of the bunch more closely together and letting the bottom grapes hang down on their strings. Glue a 1-inch twig into the center of the bunch as the stem.

HOLD EVERYTHING

For your little
collectors and their
growing collections.

PAPIER-MÂCHÉ BALLOON BOWL

Can you believe these materials combine to make a bowl? It's magic. Almost.

1 Inflate the balloon to the size that you want your bowl to be. Hold it by the knot and, beginning at the top of the balloon, coat it in 4-inch-square sections with Mod Podge using a foam brush. Place newspaper pieces on top of the Mod Podge, and then generously cover the paper with more Mod Podge. Keep covering the sides of the balloon with overlapping newspaper pieces until a bowl-like shape has formed—the less paper you add, the shallower the bowl.

2 Cover up the newspaper from step 1 using the same technique with newsprint pieces. (Applying the second layer in solid paper allows you to track your progress.) Add a third layer in newspaper, and then a fourth in newsprint. You do not need to let each layer dry in between. Let it dry completely overnight, or until it feels like a hard shell when you tap it. (I stood my balloon knot-side down in a glass bowl of a smaller diameter to dry.)

3 Pop the balloon (ta-da!), peel off the latex from inside the bowl, and throw the latex away. Cut the edge of the bowl straight across with scissors (use ones with a decorative edge to create a little flair).

4 Now paint away! You can keep it simple with a solid inside, a contrasting outside, and a bright edge, or go wild with zebra stripes, polka dots, zigzags, or splatter paint. You can even leave part of it unpainted to let the newsprint show.

MINT-TIN SUITCASE

This mini luggage is perfect for storing toy cars, crayons, or a secret stash of candy.

1 Paint the outside of your tin and let it dry. Apply a second coat of paint if needed to cover the brand label.

2 Cut four pieces of ribbon (two ½ inch wide, two ¼ inch wide) that are double the tin's height plus 3 inches.

3 To make the handles, lay the tin horizontally and glue the ½-inch ribbon to its face, spacing it evenly from each edge, curving it above the open side of the tin to make the handle, and leaving a ¼-inch overhang on the bottom. Glue the ¼-inch neutral ribbon centered on top of it. Fold the ends under the bottom of the tin, glue, and trim. Repeat on the other side. Let the glue dry.

4 Cut the points off of four mini brads with wire clippers (a job for an adult). Glue two of them to the face of the ribbon, about ¼ inch from the top edge of the tin. Repeat on the other side.

BOOKWORM ENVELOPES

Do you take the jackets off your kids' books before they inevitably tear? Here's how to put them to good use.

WHAT YOU'LL NEED

- **Envelopes**
- **Dust jackets**
- **Pen or pencil**
- **Scissors**
- **Glue stick**
- **Ruler or bone folder (optional)**

1 Carefully pull apart the seams of an envelope.

2 Trace the flattened envelope onto a dust jacket and cut it out. Make sure to position the template over your desired section of the jacket.

3 Fold your new dust-jacket envelope to match the original envelope template and glue the overlapping edges together, leaving one flap open. (You can use a ruler or a bone folder to create good flat creases for your envelopes.)

4 Use a glue stick to seal the envelope for mailing.

Use these envelopes to hold receipts, photos, memorabilia, or a note from a BFF on a bulletin board—or use one to mail grandparents a thank-you note for all the birthday books they've sent.

ROBOT BANK

Making robots might be one of the most fun crafts for kids. One, two, or three eyes—it's up to you.

WHAT YOU'LL NEED

- 2 clear plastic 8-ounce cups
- Mod Podge
- 1-inch foam brush
- Silver and turquoise glitter
- Masking tape (optional)
- Hot-glue gun
- One 26-ounce clear plastic snack container (Archer Farms snacks from Target are sold in this size)
- Electrical tape
- 2 all-purpose vinyl-coated clips
- Split flexible tubing

- One 18-ounce oatmeal container
- Scissors
- Glittered craft paper
- Tacky glue
- 15 inches of ribbon or rickrack
- 2-inch Styrofoam ball
- 6 cotton swabs
- 6 pennies
- Green and red paint
- Paintbrushes
- Black permanent marker
- Silver cord
- 1 sink strainer

No two robots (should) look alike, so feel free to go off on your own for the decoration of this craft!

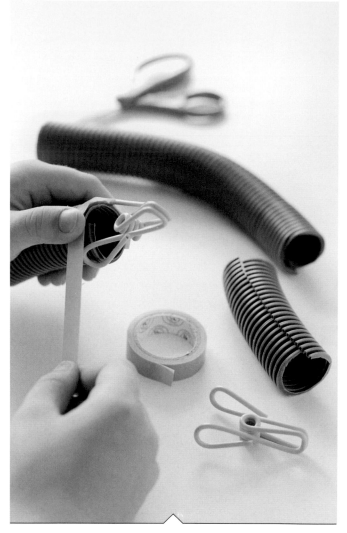

1 To make the robot's legs, coat the inside of the plastic cups with Mod Podge and pour about 2 tablespoons of silver glitter into one cup. Hold the cups together, openings facing each other, and shake to distribute the glitter. Add more glitter if needed. (You might want to tape the cups together to prevent a sparkly mess.) Once the cups are dry, shake out the excess and hot-glue them to the bottom of the snack container, open end down.

2 To make the arms, use electrical tape to attach the clips to two 4-inch pieces of tubing. Hot-glue the flat ends of the tubes to the sides of the snack container.

3 To make the head, cut off 5 inches from the top portion of the oatmeal container and discard the bottom section.

4 Cut craft paper to make a 5-inch-wide-by-14-inch-long strip. (You may have to tape two pieces together.) Wrap it around the oatmeal container, and affix it with glue. Put a line of hot glue on the inside edge of the snack container opening and place the cut end of the oatmeal container into the opening; hold it in position until the glue has set. Wrap electrical tape around the "neck" to cover any messy glue line.

5

To finish the head, cut a craft paper circle to cover the top of the oatmeal container's lid and glue ribbon or rickrack around the front edge of the lid. Cut a 1¼-inch slit through the paper and the plastic lid to make the coin slot.

6

To make the robot's antennae, coat the Styrofoam ball with Mod Podge and roll it in turquoise glitter. While it's drying, cut five cotton swabs in half and dip the soft ends in Mod Podge and then in silver glitter. Once dry, poke the glittered swabs into the Styrofoam ball. Cut both ends off of the remaining cotton swab, insert it into the bottom of the ball, and glue it to the oatmeal container lid. (You may need to secure it by poking a small hole in the lid with scissors.)

7 Paint two pennies red and four green and let them dry. With the marker, draw black dots on two green ones and glue them to the head as eyes, then glue the other four pennies to the front of the snack container in a random arrangement. Wrap silver cord around the pennies on the body once they are securely dried. Trim the cord and add a dab of glue to hold it in place.

8 Hot-glue the sink strainer to the robot's face.

SHELL COLLECTOR

Now your kids can gather up their treasures—and leave the sand where it belongs.

WHAT YOU'LL NEED

- 1 mesh produce bag
- One 5-inch embroidery hoop
- Tacky glue
- 24 inches of strap or ribbon
- Scissors
- Fishing line
- ¼-inch to ⅜-inch beads

1 Cut any labels off the bag and knot one end.

2 Fold about 1 inch of the open end of the bag around the inner ring of the embroidery hoop. Secure with glue if desired.

3 Cut a 12-inch piece of strap and glue the ends to opposite sides of the outside edge of the inner ring of the embroidery hoop to create the handle. Tighten the outer ring over the inner ring.

4 Cut a 16-inch piece of strap and glue it around the outer ring of the hoop.

5 For a decorative touch, cut 5-inch pieces of fishing line and thread eight or so beads on each, then tie the beaded strands onto the mesh bag. Trim the ends of the fishing line, if needed.

TRAY CHIC

Paint chips are an unlikely, yet super-popular, craft supply. Take your young designer to the hardware store to choose his own color palette.

WHAT YOU'LL NEED

- **Scissors**
- **Paint chips**
- **Glue**
- **Wooden toy packaging (Melissa & Doug sells many of its toy sets in these)**

1 Cut paint chips into various-sized squares and rectangles, making sure to remove any type or lettering.

2 Glue cut chips into the backs of the compartments of the wooden packaging. Do solid shapes or mix colors within each box.

3 Let the glue dry, stand the tray up, and fill it with treasures.

CRAFTY CONTAINERS

Teach kids the benefits of organization with these craft-supply towers—a cool way to keep their materials tidy.

WHAT YOU'LL NEED

- Computer, printer, and printer paper
- 8 plastic jars, in a variety of sizes (either recycled or from USPlastic.com)
- Scissors
- Clear tape
- Permanent marker
- 8 pieces of origami paper
- Pencil
- Mod Podge
- 1-inch foam brush
- Hot-glue gun

With these towers, kids can carry eight supplies in two hands!

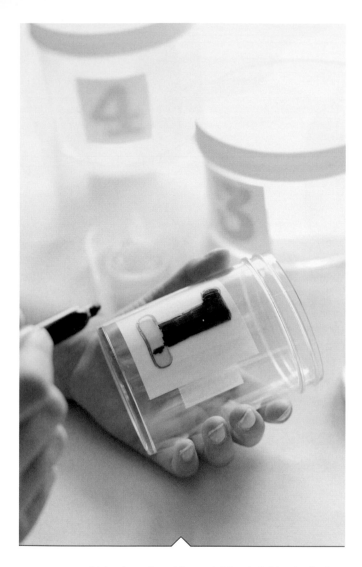

1 Print out numbers 1 through 8 in a bright color that doesn't match your marker, sized to fit on the face of the jars. Stack the jars with the largest on the bottom and the smallest on the top. Cut out the numbers and tape them to the inside of the jars in ascending order according to size. Use a permanent marker to outline the numbers on the outside of the jars, and then color them in. Try to color in continuous strokes; when you layer wet marker on top of dried marker, it tends to look streaky. Remove the paper numbers from inside the jars.

2 To decorate each lid, cut a circle of origami paper at least 1 inch wider than the diameter of the jar lid. Trace the lid in the center of the circle, then cut ¼-inch-wide fringe all the way around up to the traced line, resembling a sun.

3 Lay the paper circle facedown, coat the top of the lid with Mod Podge, then center the lid on the circle you traced. Smooth the paper onto the lid, then coat the edge of the lid with Mod Podge. Fold up the fringed part of the paper circle along this edge and smooth it out. Trim any excess paper around the edges if necessary. Once the lid is covered with paper, coat the entire thing—top and sides—with Mod Podge and set aside to dry, about 20 minutes.

4 Re-create the original stacks in descending order and hot-glue the bases of the jars to the lids they are resting on.

YARN-STRIPED VASE

There are no patterns to follow here. Just let your kids wrap their hearts out with remnants of your last knitting project.

WHAT YOU'LL NEED

- **Bottle or jar**
- **Double-stick tape**
- **Yarn in a variety of colors**
- **Scissors**
- **Tacky glue**

1 Wrap your jar or bottle with strips of double-stick tape. You can leave ½-inch spaces between the rows of tape. If you want to leave a clear band, make sure to keep that part of the bottle free of tape.

2 Starting at the bottom, wrap one color of yarn around a bottle or jar to create the first stripe. Press down where the yarn hits the tape to secure it. Some kids will want to be very neat about it, laying each wrap of yarn on top of the one below it, while others may just want to go crazy.

3 Continue wrapping the jar or bottle until it is fully covered. To change colors, cut the yarn and press the end firmly to the tape. Begin wrapping the next stripe over that end, securing the cut ends under the next few wraps.

4 Use tacky glue to secure the final end of the yarn.

Turn the page for three weaving projects!

Weaving is one of the most important—and oldest—handcrafts. Fragments of woven linens have been traced back to the prehistoric era. Everything from the clothing we wear to the rugs we walk on requires this basic technique of crisscrossing threads and yarn. It's not just soft things that are woven; baskets and wicker furniture are made this way too.

The easiest way to learn the basics of weaving is to start with paper. By cutting strips of different widths and mixing colors, you can create cool patterns with a nice, even texture. And just because paper is flat doesn't mean you can't create dimensional objects with it.

WHAT YOU'LL NEED

- Paper in a variety of colors and patterns
- Ruler
- Pencil
- Scissors

1 Using a ruler, draw a straight line across a piece of paper ¼ to 1 inch from the top edge, depending on the final project.

2 Cut slits from the bottom of the paper up to the line. You can vary the width between the slits or measure to keep them uniform.

3 From different colored papers, cut strips that are longer than the width of the slotted paper. (You can use the ruler for all strip cutting if you want to be very exact.) It's fun to mix different papers like patterned scrapbooking paper, solid construction paper, and magazine or catalog pages.

4 Take one strip and alternately weave it over and under the slits, pushing it up to the top edge. Repeat with another strip, going under where you went over, and over where you went under in the previous step. Repeat until you reach the bottom of the paper.

WEAVING PROJECTS

1

"PIXELATED" NOTEBOOK COVER

WHAT YOU'LL NEED

- One 4½-by-3½-inch notebook
- Pencil
- Graph paper
- Scissors
- Colored or patterned paper
- Clear contact paper

1 Trace the shape of the notebook onto graph paper and plot out your heart design by coloring in the squares as shown. (Two sets of two squares with three blank in between for the top row, then two sets of four squares separated by one blank space for the second row, and so on.) Keep that drawing next to you as you work.

2 Trace the notebook again on another piece of graph paper and cut vertically along the grid lines, leaving one row uncut on the top edge of the paper, above the top line of the notebook outline.

3 Cut eight strips of a third sheet of graph paper along the grid lines, and then nine strips of the same width in a contrasting colored paper.

4 Weave the top three lines with graph paper as described in the Weaving lesson on page 87. Then follow your drawing—where there are multiple colored boxes next to one another in a row, carry a colored strip over that many spaces. If there are white boxes next to each other, carry the colored paper under that many spaces. Complete the rows with no colored boxes at all, as you did on top, with strips of graph paper.

5 Cut a piece of contact paper larger than your notebook cover and smooth it over the weaving, pressing out any air bubbles. Cut it down to the size of your notebook cover, place it on top of your notebook, and then affix it with another piece of clear contact paper that wraps all the way around the edges to seal them.

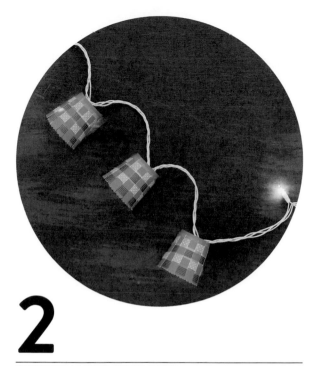

2

STRING-LIGHT SCONCES

WHAT YOU'LL NEED

- 9-ounce paper cups, one per light
- Scissors
- Scallop shears
- Ruler
- Paper in 2 colors or patterns
- Tacky glue
- String of mini twinkle lights

1 For each light, cut a paper cup in half vertically. Cut the bottom edge with scallop shears to make the cup 3 to 4 inches tall.

2 Cut about seven ½-inch-wide vertical slits in the half-cup to use as the weaving base, then weave ½-inch strips of different colored paper horizontally up the sides of the cup. Glue down the edges to secure them; trim off any excess paper.

3 Use scissors to punch a hole in the top of the shade (the bottom of the cup), and push a mini twinkle light down through it. Make sure that the base of the light is pushed all the way through the hole.

3

RECYCLED PAPER BOX

WHAT YOU'LL NEED

- 1 cereal box
- Pencil
- Ruler
- Scissors
- Paper in a variety of colors
- Tacky glue
- Colored tape

1 Cut the cereal box into two panels that are the height of the box and 4 inches wide. Fold each panel vertically in even thirds and then unfold. Cut vertical slits from the bottom of the panel, roughly ¼ to ½ inch from the top edge.

2 Weave strips of paper lengthwise up each cardboard panel until you get to the end. Add dots of glue under each loose end and trim off the excess from each side.

3 Fold a strip of colored tape over the top and bottom edge.

4 Put one panel on top of the other to make what looks like a plus sign. Recrease and fold the walls up to form a box and tape the inside corners together.

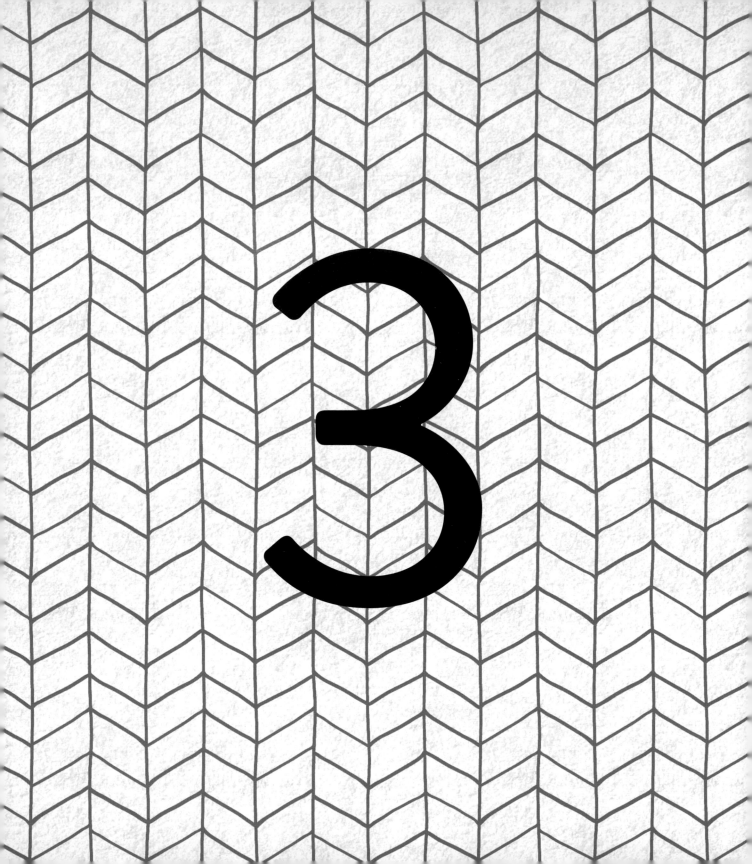

HOME SWEET HOME

Home is where
the craft is.

K-CUP DOOR CHIME

Single-cup coffeemakers rule our caffeine intake these days, so why not rescue a few cups from the trash?

WHAT YOU'LL NEED

- 7 "pods" from a single-cup coffeemaker, cleaned out
- Washi tape in 5 or 6 patterns (available from HappyTape.com)
- White paper
- Scissors
- Glue
- Thread
- 9 bells
- Small beads
- Wood Cabone ring (available at Michaels Stores)
- Ribbon

1 For each cup, cut or tear one pattern of tape into eight to twelve strips that are roughly the height of the cup and apply them vertically to the outside of the cup. Don't worry about making them neat or evenly spaced.

2 Adhere three or four strips of this same tape side by side to white paper and cut a 1-inch circle out of this covered area. Attach the circle to the bottom of the cup with glue, being careful not to cover the puncture hole that the machine made when brewing the coffee.

3 Cut a 2- to 3-foot piece of thread and tie a bell to the bottom. Thread on some beads and then a cup, stacking enough beads to prevent the cup from covering the bell. Thread on more beads, then a bell, then more beads, then a cup, and continue until you have three or four cups per strand. Repeat to make a second strand.

4 Tie both strands onto the Cabone ring, then tie a ribbon to the ring long enough to fit over a doorknob.

You can make this chime as long as you'd like—just clean out more cups!

FAMILY MESSAGE CENTER

Stop texting and leave notes the old-fashioned way.

WHAT YOU'LL NEED

- 1 clothespin per family member
- Fine-tip markers
- Self-adhesive magnets
- Large, medium, and small wood circle cutouts (available at Michaels Stores)
- Embroidery thread in the colors of your family members' hair
- Scissors
- Tacky glue
- Various ribbons
- 1 toothpick

1 Color one side of each clothespin with a marker. Adhere a magnet to the uncolored side of the clothespin.

2 Draw faces on the larger circles for adults, and the medium ones for kids. Glue to the top of the colored side of the clothespin.

3 Create hair by wrapping embroidery thread around your fingers eight to ten times: one finger for a baby's tuft, three for short hair, and four or more for longer hair. Cut the thread from the skein and twist once in the middle. Glue onto the circle at the point of the twist.

4 To create a necktie, tie a knot in a ½-inch-wide ribbon, leaving about 2 inches below the knot. Cut the bottom of the ribbon into a V shape. Glue it below the face.

5 To create a neck or hair bow, simply tie a bow with ribbon and glue it to the face.

6 To create a lollipop, draw two swirls of contrasting colors onto a small wood circle. Cut the toothpick to ¾ inch and glue it to the back of the circle. Glue to the face.

ZIP-TIE MOBILE

I fell in love with these colorful zip ties at first sight. When they met the wooden hoops, it was a match made in heaven!

WHAT YOU'LL NEED

- 4 embroidery hoops: 3-inch, 4-inch, 5-inch, and 6-inch
- Forty-two 8-inch zip ties: 14 orange, 14 yellow, and 14 pink (available at Home Depot)
- Colored cord
- Scissors

1 Fasten the two smallest inner hoop rings together with the orange zip ties. Make sure you pull them in the same direction, leaving about a 1½-inch tail on each tie.

2 Attach the 5-inch ring to the 4-inch ring with the yellow zip ties, interspersing them evenly between the orange ties.

3 Repeat, attaching the 6-inch ring to the 5-inch ring with the pink zip ties, interspersing them evenly between the yellow ties.

4 Cut 6 to 8 feet of colored cord and tie it to either end of the top ring and hang. Give the mobile a shake to evenly distribute the ties.

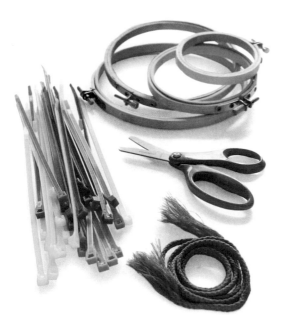

PAINTED PENNANT PORTRAIT

Silhouettes are a modern alternative to family photos—and a great opportunity to think outside the frame.

WHAT YOU'LL NEED

- Canvas drop cloth
- Scissors
- Computer, printer, and printer paper
- Profile photographs
- Pencil
- Freezer paper
- Iron
- Acrylic paints in 3 to 5 colors
- 1-inch foam brushes
- Painter's tape
- Hot-glue gun
- One ⅛-inch dowel
- String or cord (optional)

1 Cut your pennant from the drop cloth—12 inches on the short side and 16 inches on the long sides.

2 Print out a 4-inch-tall photo of a face in profile. Outline the profile with pencil. Lay the profile pencil-outline side down on the freezer paper and scribble over the outline of the silhouette to transfer the pencil mark to the freezer paper.

3 Create a stencil by cutting out the silhouette from the freezer paper and discarding the center. Lay your pennant in the direction you'd like it to hang, and iron the stencil, centered, 2 to 4 inches from the short side of the pennant. Paint the inside. Let the paint dry and pull off the freezer paper. Use painter's tape and a few colors of paint to create thick and thin stripes on either side of the silhouette. Let the stripes dry and remove the tape.

4 For a vertical pennant, glue the short side of the pennant to the dowel and hang with string. For a horizontal one, just glue the short side to one end of the dowel and display on a dresser or table in a tall cup or vase.

OFFICE-SUPPLY HOUSES

This is the perfect craft for all those mismatched envelopes crowding your stationery drawer.

WHAT YOU'LL NEED

- Envelopes
- Scissors
- Scrap paper in colors to match the envelopes (optional)
- Tacky glue
- Black adhesive-backed photo corners (about 100)
- 10 small colored paper clips
- Wire clippers
- 1 security envelope
- 1 pencil eraser
- Frame or fabric-covered foam core
- 4 straight pins

1 Open an envelope so that the flap forms a roof. Cut a 2-by-1-inch rectangle from an extra envelope or matching paper and glue it to the back of the "roof" as the chimney.

2 To create shingles, adhere photo corners along the fold of the envelope flap, pointing downward. Work your way up to the top point of the envelope, also covering the chimney. Trim any excess along the edges.

3 To make the windows, unfold four paper clips along their bends to make three-and-a-half-sided rectangles. Glue two to either side on the front of the envelope and glue the remaining two on top of them, to complete each rectangle. Unfold one more paper clip, cut two lengths that match the height of the windows using wire clippers, and glue them to the middle of the rectangles to create panes in the windows.

4 To create a door, cut a small rectangle from a security envelope, sized to fit between the windows (approximately 2 by 1½ inches). Cut the pencil eraser in half. Glue the eraser to the door as the knob. Repeat steps 1 through 4 to create a second house. Pin the envelopes to a piece of fabric-covered foam core (or frame them).

LOW-TECH LED BANNER

Did you know that any letter or number can be created from a five-by-seven grid?

WHAT YOU'LL NEED

- 1½-inch-diameter foam pipe insulation with a ½-inch opening
- Scissors
- Tacky glue
- Cardboard
- Yellow acrylic paint
- Paint roller
- 9-by-12-inch pieces of fabric or paper (1 per letter)
- Drinking straws
- Paintbrush
- String
- ¾-inch round stickers (available from InStockLabels.com)

1 Cut thirty-five 1-inch segments of foam pipe insulation.

2 Glue them into a 5-by-7 grid on an 8-by-11-inch piece of cardboard.

3 Put a dollop of paint on a spare sheet of cardboard and use a paint roller to coat the foam circles in a relatively light layer of paint. Press down with the roller to make sure paint is applied to all the foam circles.

4 Using your grid like a stamp, press it onto a piece of fabric or paper. Make sure you apply pressure so that you evenly distribute the paint. Let dry. Repeat for as many letters as you'd like to create for your banner. (Turn the page to see how it's done.)

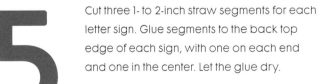

5 Cut three 1- to 2-inch straw segments for each letter sign. Glue segments to the back top edge of each sign, with one on each end and one in the center. Let the glue dry.

6 Cut one segment of the foam insulation to go between each sign and paint them yellow. Let them dry.

7 Thread string through the straw segments on the back of each letter sign, adding a painted foam segment between each letter. Allow at least a foot of string on either end of the banner for hanging.

8 Create letters by applying round stickers in the grid. (Turn the page to see how it's done.)

LED
ALPHABET

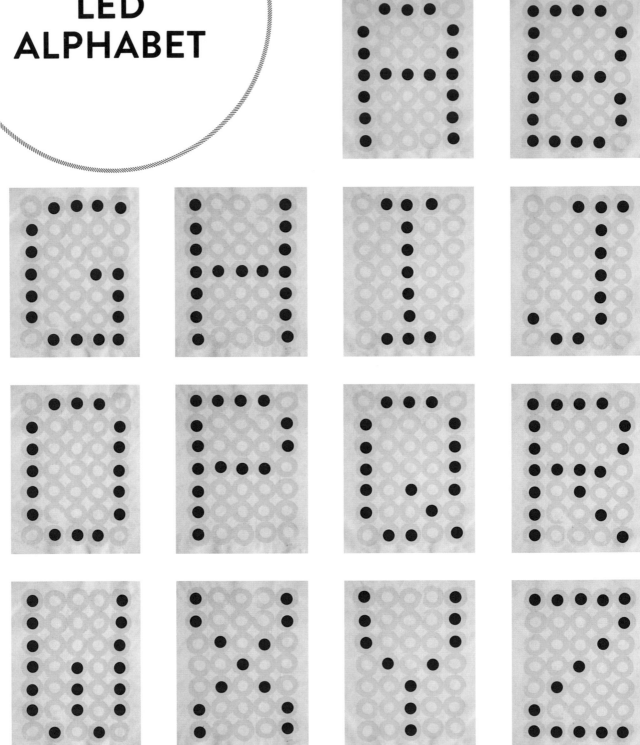

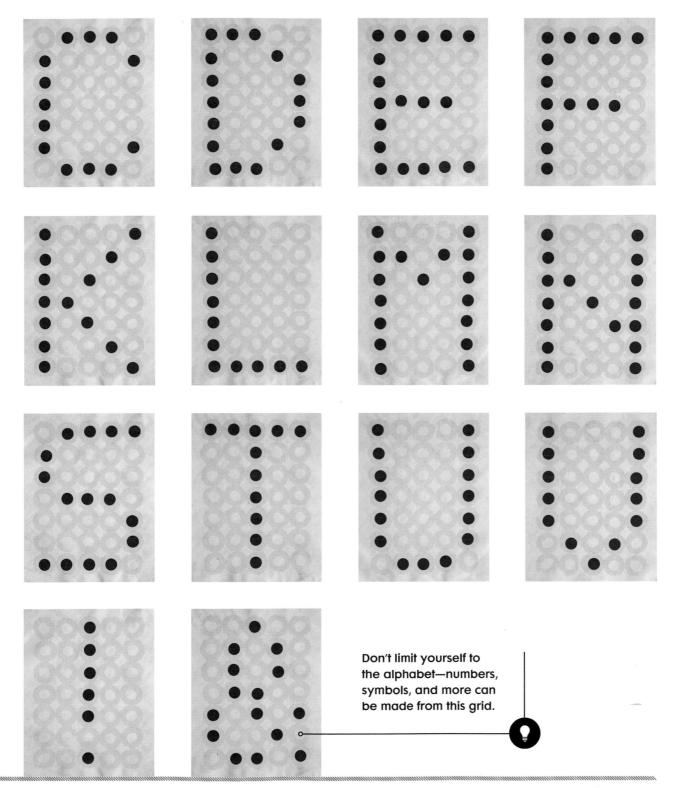

Don't limit yourself to the alphabet—numbers, symbols, and more can be made from this grid.

TEACHING TIMEPIECE

Use this chalkboard clock to help kids learn to tell time. Or hang it on the wall, set to their bedtime (hint, hint)!

WHAT YOU'LL NEED

- One 12-inch round cardboard cake circle
- 12 drink lids
- Chalkboard paint
- 1-inch foam brush
- ¾-inch number stickers
- Pencil
- One 12-inch square of oilcloth
- Scissors
- One 7-inch plate
- Tacky glue
- 38 inches of rope, plus extra for hanging
- Chalk

1 Paint the cardboard cake circle and the centers of the drink lids with chalkboard paint. Let them dry.

2 Affix number stickers to the centers of the drink lids, 1 through 12.

3 Trace the cardboard circle onto the back of the oilcloth and cut it out. Trace the plate in the center of the oilcloth circle, cut it out, and save the center cutout in your remnants bin for a future project.

4 Glue the remaining oilcloth ring to the painted side of the cardboard circle, and then glue the drink lids on top of the oilcloth. To help you space them evenly, begin with 12, 6, 3, and 9 o'clock.

5 Glue rope around the edge of the cardboard ring and create a 10- to 12-inch loop at the top to hang the clock.

6 Use chalk to draw the clock's hands.

PHOTO FRAME FAMILY TREE

The recessed lids of Play-Doh containers easily transform into brightly colored picture frames.

WHAT YOU'LL NEED

- **18- to 24-inch-long sticks**
- **White paint**
- **1-inch foam brush**
- **Scissors**
- **Black-and-white portrait photographs**
- **Play-Doh lids (one for each family member)**
- **Glue**
- **Styrofoam**
- **1 cup or vase**
- **Fun-Tak (available at office-supply stores)**

1 Paint the sticks and let them dry.

2 Measure the recessed part of Play-Doh lids, then cut the faces from photographs to fit inside the lids. Affix the photos onto the lids with glue.

3 Fit a piece of Styrofoam snugly in the cup, and push the sticks down into it.

4 Use Fun-Tak to attach the lids to the sticks.

You may want to make one or more circle templates to match the size(s) of your lids, to trace around the photos.

CONFETTI LAMP

Spice up a plain lampshade with an explosion of confetti.

WHAT YOU'LL NEED

- **1 package of tissue paper circle confetti (available from KnotAndBow.com)**
- **Tacky glue**
- **Lampshade**
- **Lamp base**

1 Glue the paper circles to the lampshade. Play with the design—you can group colors together; create a falling effect by grouping them together at the top and spreading them out toward the bottom; or create different patterns like stripes, circles, or chevrons.

2 Place the shade on the lamp base and enjoy!

If you have a large circle paper punch (up to 1½ inches in diameter), you can create your own confetti from regular tissue paper.

Turn the page for three projects using fringe!

Fringe has reinvented itself in the fashion world at least once every decade for the last hundred years, from Native American garb to renegade Western, dapper flapper to happy hippie. And it appears on just about every other Halloween costume year after year. (Come October 31, you'll see what I mean.)

Fringing isn't limited to just clothing: use it to decorate accessories in your home such as lampshades and pillows, spice up a plain garland, or create your own piñata. Best of all, all it takes is the ability to wield a pair of scissors!

WHAT YOU'LL NEED

- **Paper, fabric, or tissue paper**
- **Scissors**

Cut parallel strips about the same width and length in paper or fabric, making sure to leave the top edge intact. When using a thin or fragile material like tissue or crepe paper, fold the paper a few times so you can cut through more than one layer at once.

FRINGING PROJECTS

1

PETITE PIÑATA

WHAT YOU'LL NEED

- 1 small box, about 3 inches square (the kind that holds a pot of facial cream is ideal)
- Confetti or a small, lightweight gift
- Tissue paper in a variety of colors
- Scissors
- Tape
- String

1 Cut off the bottom of the box. Put the confetti or small gift inside the box, then wrap the box in tissue paper like you would a present, covering the open side.

2 Fold 1-inch-long strips of tissue paper and fringe them. Tape them around the box, covering the sides.

3 Make a tassel by fringing three more strips of tissue paper, spacing your cuts about ⅛ inch apart. Cut these three strips into 3-inch-long pieces, stack, and tape a 4-inch-long string in the center, perpendicular to the fringed strips. Roll the strips lengthwise and wrap a piece of clear tape around the top. Wrap string around the tape to cover the end and knot.

4 Carefully poke the end of the tassel's string through the bottom of the box and seal with clear tape.

5 Holding the piñata in one hand, pull the tassel to reveal the surprise inside!

2

CUPCAKE-LINER CARNATION

WHAT YOU'LL NEED

- 2 cupcake liners
- Scissors
- 1 drinking straw
- Green tape

1 Place the cupcake liners face-to-face, with the color or pattern on the outside. Fringe only the ruffled part of the liners, stopping when you reach the center flat circle.

2 Fold the liners in half, then in half again. Roll this "quarter circle" from the bottom and push the point you've created snugly into the drinking straw.

3 Tear off a 2-inch piece of green tape and center the tape on the shaft of the straw. Fold the ends back in on themselves and adhere them next to the straw.

4 Bend the neck of the straw to angle your flowers slightly outward.

3

FLASHY FELT NECKLACE

WHAT YOU'LL NEED

- Felt
- Pinking shears
- Tacky glue
- String
- Scissors
- Beads and sequins

1 Fold a 3-inch piece of felt in half and cut a half leaf shape on the fold, about 1 inch at its widest point, with pinking shears.

2 Glue the felt leaf over the center of an 18-inch string, adding extra glue as needed so it stays closed.

3 With regular scissors, fringe the felt, using the pinking shear points as a guide to keep the fringes even.

4 Alternate threading beads and sequins on either side of the fringed felt. Tie at the back.

PLAYTIME

Making toys can
be as much fun as
playing with them.

CUSTOM-PAINTED BLOCKS

Give your child total control over color and pattern, or lack thereof, and she'll play with these blocks forever.

WHAT YOU'LL NEED

- 2-inch and/or 1-inch wooden blocks (available from CreateForLess.com)
- Newspaper
- Acrylic paint in a variety of colors
- 1-inch foam brushes

1 Lay the blocks out on newspaper. Choose one color and paint either an entire side or half a side that color. Before moving on to the next color, complete multiple blocks with your first color of paint. Let dry.

2 Turn each block and add the next color. Continue until the blocks are painted to your liking. Let all of your blocks dry completely.

3 Now build the world's tallest skyscraper.

HOMEMADE MEMORY GAME

Put your kids' drawings to use by crafting a tailor-made memory game.

WHAT YOU'LL NEED

- **20 to 30 plain white coasters (available from Amazon.com)**
- **Crayons, markers, or colored pencils**
- **Computer, scanner, and printer, or color copier**
- **Card stock**
- **Scissors**
- **Glue stick**
- **2½-inch circle stickers (available from Paper-Source.com)**
- **Craft paper**
- **1½-inch paper punch**
- **1 coaster caddy**

1 Have your child draw ten to fifteen different pictures on the coasters.

2 Scan and print or color copy each of the drawings onto card stock and cut them out to match the size and shape of the coaster. Glue the duplicate drawings to blank coasters.

3 Center a sticker on the back side of all the coasters. Punch circles out of craft paper using the paper punch and glue them on top of the stickers.

4 Store the coasters in the coaster caddy. To play the game, shuffle the coasters and place them facedown. Take turns flipping over two coasters to find a match. If you succeed, keep both coasters. If not, turn both back over. The player with the most matches at the end of the game wins.

You can decorate the backs any way you'd like (or not at all). Just make sure they are all the same!

TOTALLY TUBULAR TRAIN

Help your preschooler make this train, and then let him decorate it any way he choo-chooses.

WHAT YOU'LL NEED

- 1 paper towel tube
- Scissors
- 1 small jar lid
- Tacky glue
- 1 raisin box, with one end open
- Blue, black, and silver paint
- Paintbrushes
- Gold sequins
- 1 wooden spool
- Hole punch (⅛- or ¼-inch)
- 6 toothpicks
- 12 large buttons
- 12 beads
- One 12-inch piece of yarn

1 Cut the paper towel tube into three equal pieces, then trim one piece down about ½ inch. To create the locomotive (the front, engine car), glue the short tube to the top of the jar lid, and glue the bottom of the jar lid to a wide side of the raisin box, open side down. Let the glue dry.

2 Paint all three train parts blue and let them dry. Add silver and black stripes, or whatever decoration you'd like. Glue sequins along the sides of the train. Paint the wooden spool black, let it dry, and attach it to the front of the train as its smokestack.

3 Punch two holes about ½ inch from the tube ends at the front and back of each "cargo car" tube and on the front end of the locomotive. Then punch two holes on the narrow sides of the raisin box, about ¼ inch from the bottom.

4 Push a toothpick through each set of holes, slip a button on each end, then glue beads to the end of the toothpicks to keep the buttons in place. Glue the yarn along the bottoms of all the cars to connect them.

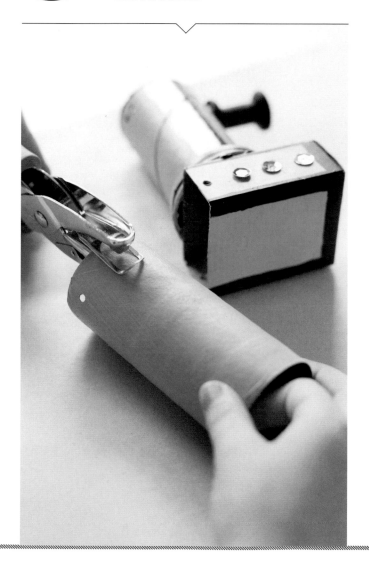

UP, UP, AND AWAY HOT-AIR BALLOON

Kids obsess over toy planes, trains, and automobiles, but it's time the hot-air balloon had her moment in the sun.

WHAT YOU'LL NEED

- Parchment paper
- Scissors
- 1 small yogurt cup
- Mod Podge
- 1-inch foam brush
- Twine
- Tacky glue
- ⅛-inch hole punch
- Two 18-inch pieces cloth stem wire, 20 gauge
- Turquoise fishnet stockings (available from WeLoveColors.com)
- One 6-inch white paper lantern (available from PearlRiver.com)
- Turquoise yarn
- Ribbon (2 patterns that are ⅜ inch wide, 1 solid that is ¼ inch wide)
- 4 white buttons
- 1 tea bag
- Hot-glue gun

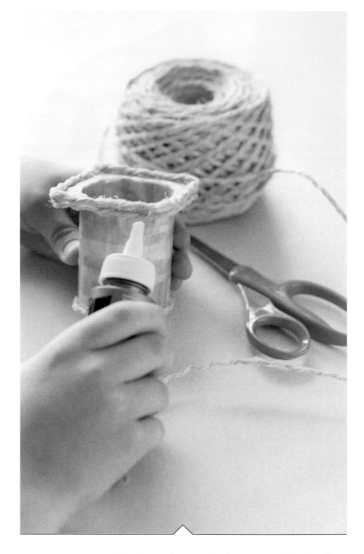

1 To create the basket, cut the parchment paper into small pieces, no bigger than 1 inch square. Apply a thin layer of Mod Podge on one side of the yogurt cup and cover the cup with the paper. Apply more Mod Podge over the covered surface. Repeat for the next three sides and the top. Let dry.

2 Glue two pieces of twine around the top lip of the yogurt cup. Glue twine around the bottom edge of the cup as well.

3 Punch a hole in each corner of the cup. Thread one piece of wire down through one hole, then up through the hole on the same side of the cup. Pull the wire until the two ends are even. Repeat on the other side of the cup.

4 Cut about a 6-inch piece from the middle of the leg of the fishnet stockings and slip it over the lantern so that it stretches from top to bottom. Glue a piece of yarn around the top and bottom opening of the lantern to cover the raw fishnet edge.

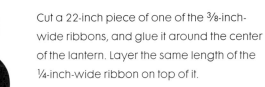

5 Cut a 22-inch piece of one of the ⅜-inch-wide ribbons, and glue it around the center of the lantern. Layer the same length of the ¼-inch-wide ribbon on top of it.

6 Glue the four ends of the wire to the ribbon, evenly spaced around the lantern.

7

Cut a 26-inch piece of the other ⅜-inch-wide ribbon. Glue ribbon to one point where the wire meets the lantern. Twist the ribbon once, then glue on top of next wire point, dropping the ribbon swag about 1 inch. Repeat three times, until the two ends of the ribbon meet. Glue buttons on top of where you glued the swag.

8

To make the sandbag, fold the tea bag in half vertically and hot-glue it. Then fold it in half horizontally and hot-glue it. Wrap the string around the top part of the bag about four times and glue the string to the inside of the yogurt cup.

BOTTLE ROCKET

Look no farther than your shower caddy to make a toy that's out of this world!

WHAT YOU'LL NEED

- 1 kid's sock
- 1 liquid soap bottle
- Hot-glue gun
- Red felt
- Scissors
- Tacky glue
- Aluminum foil tape (available at Home Depot)
- White cardboard
- 1 cardboard wrapping paper tube
- Red, yellow, and orange yarn

2 Cut two 2-inch circles from the felt and glue them to the front of the bottle about an inch apart from each other. Cut two 1-inch circles from aluminum foil tape and affix them to the middle of the felt circles.

1 Slip the sock over the bottle. Fold the bottom of the sock under the bottle, trimming it if the excess is more than 2 inches. Hot-glue the sock to the bottom of the bottle.

3

Cut four matching "fin" shapes out of the cardboard, about 5 inches tall, and hot-glue them to the side bottom edges of the covered bottle.

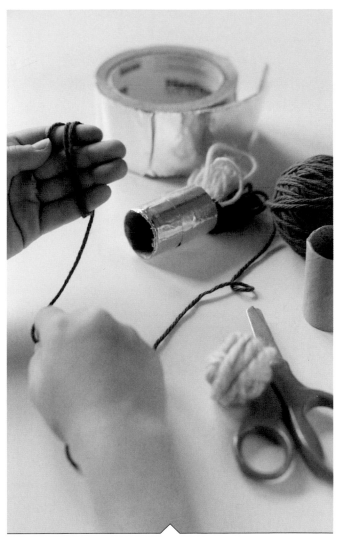

4

Cut two 2-inch lengths of the wrapping paper tube and cover them in foil tape. Wind the red yarn around your hand (about ten times for an average six-year-old's hand), slip it off, and glue the wad inside one of the tubes. Repeat using the yellow and orange yarns, then repeat this process with the other tube. Glue the tubes to the bottom of the bottle rocket.

BANGIN' BONGO DRUMS

Now your kid can really march to the beat of his very own drum.

WHAT YOU'LL NEED

- One 42-ounce oatmeal container
- Scissors
- White paint
- 1-inch foam brush
- Blue- and green-tinted clear plastic vinyl (available from TheFabricExchange.com)
- ⅛- or ¼-inch hole punch
- 2 rubber bands
- Green and orange stretchy lanyard (available at Michaels Stores)
- Tacky glue
- 2 cups of dried orange lentils

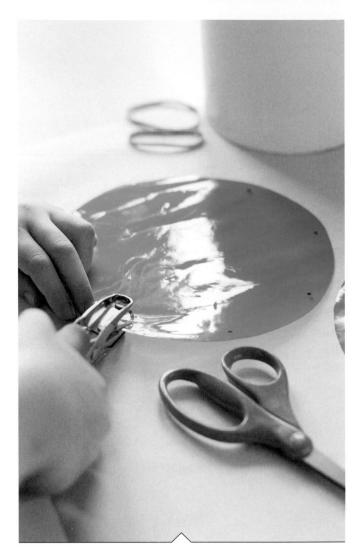

1 Cut the oatmeal container in half. This will make two drums. Paint the inside and outside of each drum. Let them dry.

2 For each drum, cut two 7-inch circles from one color of the vinyl. Punch eight evenly spaced holes around each circle. Center one vinyl circle on top of the cylinder and secure with a rubber band. Flip the cylinder over and secure the second vinyl circle, making sure to stagger the holes with those of the first one.

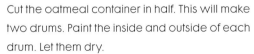

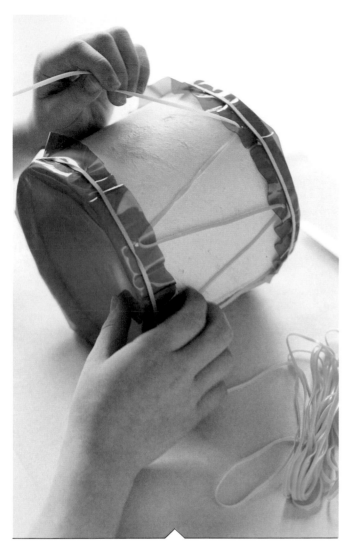

3 Cut a 4-foot-piece of lanyard and weave it in and out of the holes, from top to bottom. Pull taut and knot the two ends together. Remove the rubber bands.

4 Squeeze glue into a triangle shape in between each lanyard line and cover with dried lentils. Rock on.

ABC FLASH CARDS

Turn tabbed letter index cards into an alphabet and geometry lesson.

- **Craft foam**
- **Scissors**
- **Five 1-inch-wide drink lids**
- **Glue**
- **Alphabet tabbed index cards**
- **Ink pads**
- **Pen**

1 Cut a circle, a square, a diamond, a triangle, and a thin rectangle from craft foam, making sure that each shape is less than 1 inch in diameter. Glue them to the tops of the drink lids to make stamps.

2 Use the stamps to create pictures on the index cards, matching the first letter of the object to the letter on the card you are using. For example, three circles could become balloons for the letter B.

3 Use a pen to draw fine lines when needed.

DOLLY'S OVEN-MITT SLEEPING BAG

Instead of sewing a sleeping bag for your child's lovey, decorate one that's already made—an oven mitt.

WHAT YOU'LL NEED

- Craft foam
- Scissors
- Glue
- Cardboard
- Blue and red acrylic or fabric paint
- One 6½-by-8½-inch oven mitt (mine was made by Kane Home)
- ⅜-inch adhesive felt tabs
- One 4-by-6-inch muslin bag (available from ElementsBath AndBody.com)
- 10 to 12 cotton balls
- Red yarn

1 To make your homemade stamps, cut one 1-inch and one 1½-inch right triangle from craft foam and glue them to small cardboard squares. Cut the cardboard to match the triangular foam shapes.

2 Dip the larger triangle in the blue paint and stamp it onto the oven mitt in a quiltlike pattern as shown. Let dry, about 30 minutes.

3 Dip the smaller triangle in the red paint, and fill in the open places of the pattern. Let dry.

4 Stick felt tabs at the intersections of the triangles' points.

5 To make the pillow, stuff the muslin bag with cotton balls, and glue the edge of the bag together.

6 Glue a piece of red yarn around the open end of the bag and tie a knot. Trim any excess yarn.

Just like when you're creating a real quilt, draw out your design on paper before starting.

FAIRGROUND GOODIES

We all have a favorite carnival food that we wish would never run out. Make your own out of paper and it will never go stale.

WHAT YOU'LL NEED

- Brown paper grocery bags
- Tacky glue
- White, red, and yellow paint
- Paintbrushes
- 1 brown paper lunch bag
- Newspaper
- 1 popsicle stick
- 1 square cracker box
- Scallop scissors
- Red crayon
- Resealable gallon-size plastic bag
- Packing peanuts
- 10 to 12 cotton balls
- Cookie sheet lined with wax paper
- Spray bottle
- Blue food coloring
- Washi tape (available from HappyTape.com)
- Cardboard
- Magazines

PRETZEL

1 Cut a grocery bag into 3-inch-wide strips and glue them together to make a 24-inch-long piece.

2 Roll and crumple the strip into a rope shape, being sure to keep any labels or writing on the inside.

3 Fold the tube into a U shape, then bend the ends toward the bottom of the U, twist them, and glue them down, crisscrossed. (You may want to put the pretzel under a medium-heavy book until it dries.)

4 Paint white dots on as the salt.

CANDY APPLE

1 Cut about 3 inches off the top of the lunch bag and discard the top piece.

2 Fill the bag with newspaper and glue it shut around the Popsicle stick. Shape the bag into a round apple shape.

3 Paint the outside of the bag red and let it dry.

POPCORN

1 Unfold the cracker box. Measure 7 to 8 inches from the bottom folds to where the top of the popcorn box will be, and cut a line straight across with scallop scissors.

2 Paint the inside surface (nonprinted side) of the box white. Let it dry.

3 Color red stripes vertically on the painted side of the box with the crayon.

4 Reassemble and glue the box so that the decorated side is on the outside.

5 To make the popcorn, squeeze a quarter-size dollop of yellow paint into the resealable bag, add enough packing peanuts to fill the cracker box, and shake. Start with a little paint; you can always add more.

6 Set the popcorn out to dry on a sheet of newspaper. Once the popcorn is dry, fill your box.

COTTON CANDY

1 Unroll about ten cotton balls onto the wax-paper-lined cookie sheet.

2 Fill the spray bottle with water and about ten drops of blue food coloring. Spray the cotton and let it dry.

3 Pull the cotton apart slightly and make a wad to form the shape of the cotton candy.

4 Cut a circle with a 12-inch diameter from a grocery bag. Cut this circle into four quarters. Take one of these quarter-circles, roll it into a cone, and glue. Cut across the top, open end to make a straight edge.

5 Stripe the paper cone with washi tape.

6 Fill with cotton candy.

PIZZA

1 Cut a triangle from cardboard, with two long sides of about 7 inches and a short side of about 5 inches. The short side of the triangle (the crust side of the pizza) should be slightly rounded.

2 Give your pizza some tomato sauce by painting the cardboard red and let it dry.

3 To make the crust, roll and crumple a 4-inch-wide-by-7-inch-long strip of brown grocery bag into a tubelike shape and glue it across the rounded edge of the pizza. Trim or glue any excess underneath.

4 Paint a 10-by-10-inch piece of newspaper yellow on both sides. Once it's dry, fringe 1/4-inch strips of the paper (see the Fringing lesson on page 120) and then cut across to make tiny strips, about 1 inch long.

5 Cut pepperoni and peppers (or whatever toppings you like) from magazine pages in the appropriate colors.

6 Brush watered-down glue (in about a 1-to-1 ratio) onto the cardboard, then sprinkle the "cheese" on top. Glue the toppings on top of the cheese.

NEWSPAPER PIRATE SHIP

Make this vessel out of the sports section, the funny pages, or the front-page news. Whatever floats your boat.

WHAT YOU'LL NEED

- Newspaper
- Scissors
- Clear contact paper
- Hot-glue gun
- 1 large wooden bead
- 1 tongue depressor
- 2 bamboo skewers
- Tacky glue
- 3 small wooden beads
- 2 pieces of black-and-white patterned paper
- ⅛-inch hole punch
- ½-inch-wide ribbon
- String

1 Cut an 11½-by-15-inch piece of newspaper and cover one side with clear contact paper.

2 Fold it into an origami boat (see instructions, pages 162–163), being sure to make the first fold with the contact paper side in.

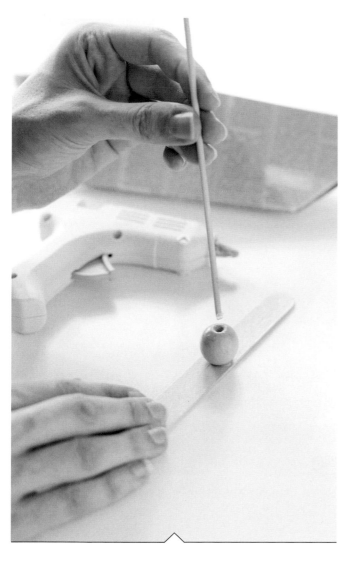

3 Hot-glue the large bead to the center of the tongue depressor and hot-glue a skewer into the middle of the bead.

4 Cut the tip off of the paper peak that pokes out of the center of the boat and insert the skewer through that hole. Glue the tongue depressor to the bottom edges of the boat.

5 Break or cut another skewer so that one side is about ½ inch shorter than the other, and glue the shorter piece into the front crease (the bow) and the longer one into the back crease (the stern). Glue a small wooden bead to the exposed end of each skewer.

6 Cut two rectangles from patterned paper, one 3 by 5 inches and one 2½ by 4 inches, and punch two holes centered about ⅛ inch from the top and bottom edges. Slip these patterned-paper sails over the center skewer, beginning with the larger one, and glue a bead on the top point.

7. Cut nine 1- to 2-inch pieces of ribbon and an 18-inch piece of string. Fold the ribbons over the string, evenly spaced, and glue them back-to-back. Trim them into triangular flag shapes.

8 Attach the string to the ends of all three skewers, tying it to the skewer on the back of the boat, then gluing it to the top of the sails, and finally tying to the skewer at the front of the boat. Secure at bow and stern with a dab of glue.

ORIGAMI BOAT

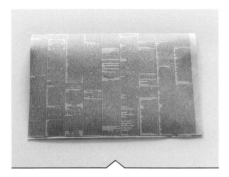

1 Fold the paper in half downward, making sure the contact paper side is facing in.

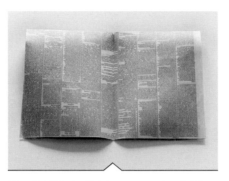

2 Fold it in half sideways and unfold to create a crease.

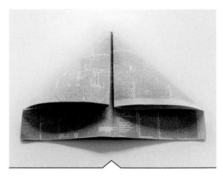

3 Fold the top corners in toward the crease.

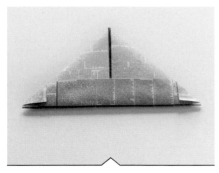

7 Fold the corners forward around to the front.

8 Pull the two layers of newspaper on the bottom edge of the triangle apart, pushing the triangle's bottom points together. It should naturally start to pop into a square shape.

9 Fold the upper layer of the left bottom corner upward.

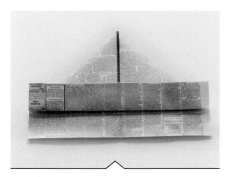

4 Fold the top layer of the bottom part up.

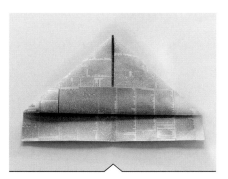

5 Fold the corners around the back.

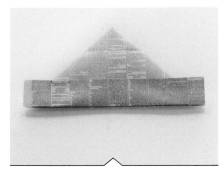

6 Fold the other bottom layer backward.

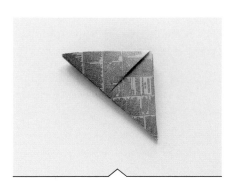

10 Fold the remaining left bottom corner backward.

11 As you did in step 8, pull apart the two layers of newspaper on the flat edge of the triangle and push the bottom points together to form a square.

12 Pull apart the top folds at the top right corner of the square to make a boat.

GOLF-TEE TOP

Make custom colors for these spinners by mixing food coloring and store-bought clay.

WHAT YOU'LL NEED

- **Crayola Model Magic (available at Michaels Stores)**
- **Food coloring**
- **1 golf tee**
- **Tacky glue**
- **1 wooden bead**

1 Break off walnut-size chunks of Model Magic and add a drop of food coloring to each. Mix, adding more food coloring until you achieve your desired color. (Yes, prepare to have messy hands.)

2 Flatten the clay into disklike shapes, spheres, and pyramids. Stack on the golf tee, then remove, keeping the pieces together.

3 Let the pieces dry (per package instructions), still as one unit, and then slip them back onto the tee and secure at the top and bottom with a dab of glue.

4 Glue the bead to the top of the tee.

Sandwich pieces of string between two layers of Model Magic for a fun look.

OUT-OF-THE-BOX VILLAGE

Take a closer look at graph and notebook papers. Do you see what I see? Bricks, shingles, and siding?

WHAT YOU'LL NEED

- **Food boxes (crackers, pasta, cereal)**
- **Notebook and graph papers**
- **Clear tape**
- **Scissors**
- **Metal brads**
- **Green graph paper**
- **Paper towel tubes**

1 For each building, wrap a box in lined notebook or graph paper like a present and seal with tape.

2 To create the door, cut a rectangle about half the height of the box from a contrasting paper and press a brad through where the doorknob would be. Tape the door to the front bottom edge of the box.

3 To give the building a roof, cut a corner off of another box of similar width or larger, wrap it in graph paper, and tape it onto the top of the other box. A triangle can be tricky to wrap, so you may need an extra piece of graph paper to cover any bare spots. Repeat to build your town.

4 Crumple up green graph paper to create shrubbery in front of your houses. Press a few wads of it into paper towel tubes to make trees.

**Turn the page for three
mosaic projects!**

Tracing back over four thousand years, mosaic is the art of creating images and patterns with a collection of like pieces of colored glass, stone, tile, or other materials. You can see mosaics in the oldest of churches and temples, under your feet on outdoor walkways, on the backsplashes of many kitchens, and even on the walls of New York City subway stations.

Kids can learn the basics of mosaic by cutting or tearing any material into small pieces and then gluing it within a defined space. The smaller the material is cut, the more intricate the image or design. It's a craft that teaches patience and precision, and the results can be really spectacular.

WHAT YOU'LL NEED

- Mounting surface (best to start with paper)
- Pencil
- Cuttable or rippable material (such as paper, fabric, or craft foam) in 2 colors
- Scissors
- Glue

1 With a pencil, draw a shape, letter, or picture onto your mounting surface.

2 Cut or tear the two colors of your material into small pieces.

3 Glue one color within your shape, and one color outside the shape. You may have to cut or tear pieces as you go to make them fit within your design.

MOSAIC PROJECTS

1

PIECE-FUL TOTE BAG

WHAT YOU'LL NEED

- Colored tape
- One 8-by-10-inch cloth bag
- Felt in 5 colors
- Tacky glue

1 Create the outline of a shape with colored tape on the surface of the cloth bag.

2 Cut felt into small pieces. Glue the pieces within the taped line, moving from one vertical band of color to the next, and let the glue dry.

3 Remove the tape.

2

STICKY-NOTE MASTERPIECE

WHAT YOU'LL NEED

- Cardboard
- 1 frame
- Pencil
- Sticky notes in a variety of colors

1 Cut a piece of cardboard to fit inside the frame.

2 Draw a shape or picture on the cardboard with a pencil.

3 Tear sticky notes to fill in the shapes, making sure to retain the adhesive part. Ready for a new design? Pull off the sticky notes, erase the pencil lines, and begin again!

3

MAGNETIC PENCIL HOLDER

WHAT YOU'LL NEED

- Scissors
- Adhesive-backed magnetic strip
- Paper in a variety of colors and patterns
- 1 metal coffee can

1 Cut a 4- to 6-inch piece of adhesive-backed magnetic strip.

2 Pull off the backing paper and press it onto a piece of colored paper, smoothing it to prevent air bubbles.

3 Cut the covered magnetic strip into shapes. Repeat with other colors or patterns of paper, and then arrange them on the coffee can. (You can store the extra pieces inside the can.)

READY TO WEAR

What better way to
show off your crafts
than to wear them?

A+ GRADUATION CAP

What is more fitting than the alphabet to top off a preschool graduation cap?

WHAT YOU'LL NEED

- One 7-inch square piece of cardboard
- Graph paper
- Tape
- 4 to 5 ink pads
- 1-inch letter stamps (available from EducationalInsights.com)
- 1 paper party hat
- Scissors
- 2 pom-poms (learn how to make your own on page 57)
- Hot-glue gun
- String
- Tacky glue

1 Wrap the cardboard in graph paper and seal with tape.

2 Using the letter stamps, create patterns on the graph paper. (Turn the page for some fun suggestions!)

3 Cut the paper party hat to 2 inches tall and discard the pointed section. Hot-glue the underside of the graduation cap board to the top of the hat section and let it dry.

4 To make the tassel, glue the pom-poms to 5- and 7-inch-long pieces of string respectively and glue the strings to the center of the stamped graph paper.

A

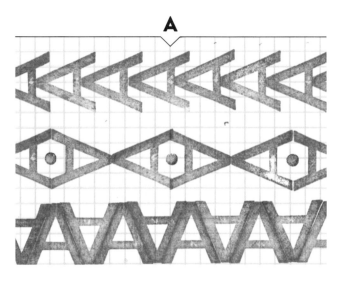

H

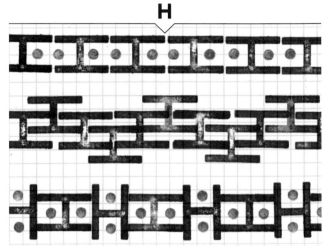

R

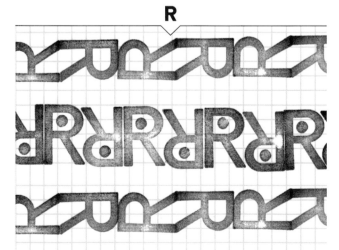

S

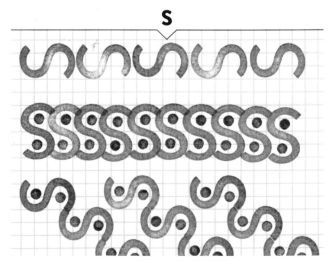

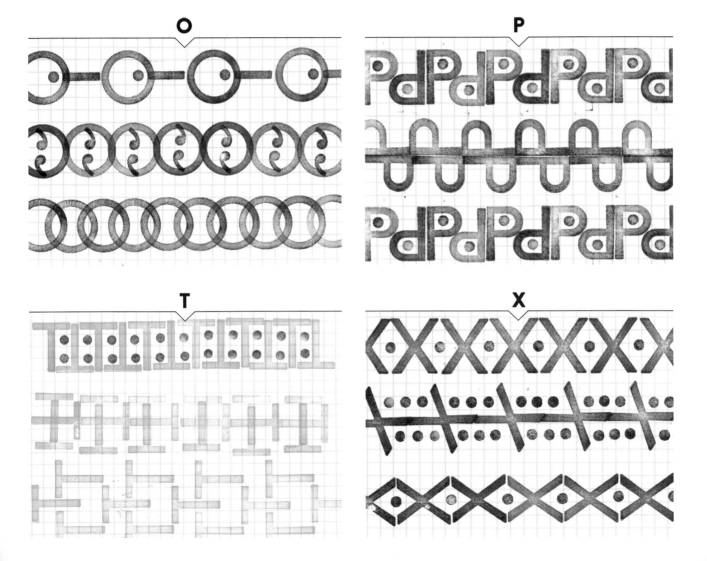

FAIRY WREATH

Pixies from the forest are notoriously crafty little creatures! If they can't find flowers, they make them.

WHAT YOU'LL NEED

- Bark-covered wire (available at Michaels Stores)
- Wire cutters
- Crepe paper sheets in three shades of pink (available from CarteFini.com)
- 15 pipe cleaners
- Tacky glue
- Scissors
- 9 rubber bands
- Clothespins or binder clips
- Glitter glue

1 Create a head wreath by making a double circle of wire large enough to fit your child's head, wrapping the ends together to close. Set aside.

2 Cut a 9-by-6-inch piece of crepe paper and five 9-inch lengths of pipe cleaner. Glue the pipe cleaners vertically down the paper, evenly spaced.

3 Cut through the pipe cleaners and crepe paper horizontally, creating three separate 3-by-6-inch pieces. This will make three flowers. Repeat steps 2 and 3 using the two other colors of crepe paper to make a total of nine flowers.

4 Roll each section of crepe paper into a tubelike shape with the pipe cleaners on the outside and glue the edges together.

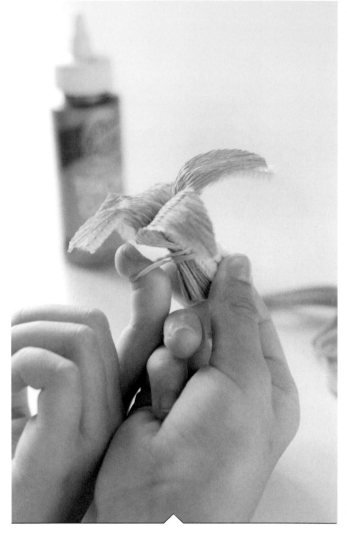

5 To make the petals of each flower, cut a 1-inch slit vertically between each pipe cleaner. Fold the five sections back to create a flower shape. Trim each bent piece into a point to resemble a petal. Trim the base of each flower to ½ to 1 inch.

6 Wrap a rubber band snugly around the base of the flower, then squirt glue into the center. Leave the base wrapped in the rubber band until the glue is dry.

Glue flowers around the wreath in small bunches. (Clip them to the wire with clothespins or binder clips to keep them in place while the glue is drying.)

8 Squeeze a dot of glitter glue in the center of each flower and let it dry.

HARDWARE-STORE ACCESSORIES

Mix and match colors to make these stylish baubles—kids will love to trade them with their friends.

WHAT YOU'LL NEED

- Round, square, or hexagonal washers and nuts
- Acrylic paint in various colors
- Paintbrushes
- Clear nail polish
- 0.5-mm Chinese knotting cord in various colors (available from TanglesNKnots.com)
- Tape
- Scissors

If you don't have Chinese knotting cord, embroidery thread will work just fine.

1 Paint the washers and nuts various colors and let them dry. You may need two coats. Seal the paint by applying a layer of clear nail polish to each washer and nut. Let them dry.

2 For each bracelet, cut the knotting cord into two 20-inch and two 12-inch pieces.

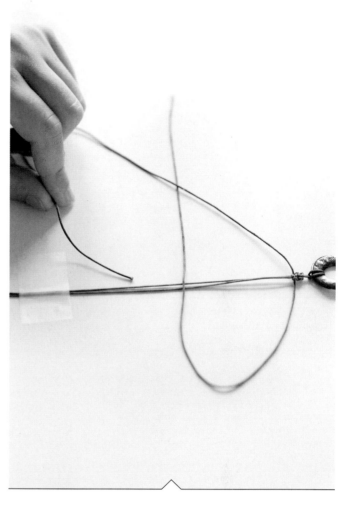

3 Fold one of the 12-inch pieces in half, thread the loop through a washer (or nut), fold it over the washer, and pull the rest of the cord through the loop. Repeat on the other side of the washer. Tape the two attached strands to a tabletop to make it easier to braid the cords.

4 To begin knotting one side of the bracelet, center a 20-inch cord under the two middle strands. Bend the right half of the cord over the middle strands, forming a "p" shape.

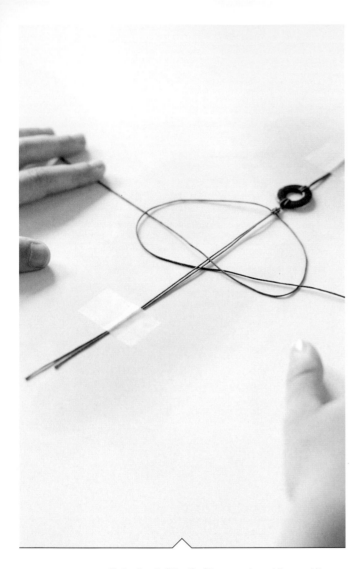

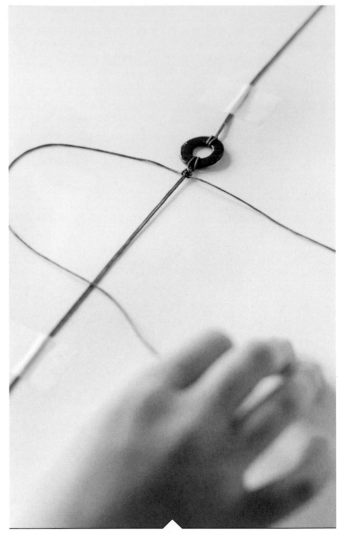

5 Take the left half of the cord and thread it under the right half of the cord and middle strands, then pull it through the open space of the "p" in a diagonal motion. Pull tightly with both sides of the cord and slide the knot up to the washer.

6 Now fold the left side of the cord over the middle strands (creating a backward "p").

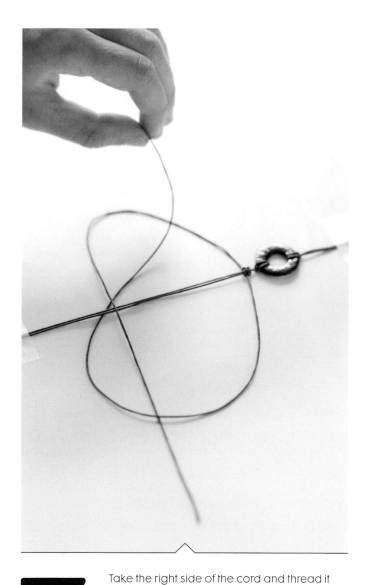

7 Take the right side of the cord and thread it under the left side of the cord and middle strands, then pull it up through the open space of the backward "p" in a diagonal motion. Pull tightly up to the last knot and repeat the steps until you've reached the desired length. Knot the left and right sides of the cord together. Repeat steps 4 through 7 with the cord on the other side of the washer.

8 Tie onto your child's wrist, letting the excess dangle. Repeat steps 2 through 8 to make as many bracelets as you'd like.

REVERSIBLE FELT CROWN

Sometimes you feel like a dot, sometimes you don't.

WHAT YOU'LL NEED

- White wool felt (available from MagicCabin.com)
- Scissors
- ½- to ¾-inch-wide metallic velvet ribbon
- Tacky glue
- Acrylic paint
- 1 wine-bottle cork

1 Cut a strip of wool felt long enough to fit the circumference of your child's head. The width of the piece should be between 4 and 6 inches. Cut crown points along one edge.

2 To create the crisscrossed side, glue ribbon from the top of the first point down to the bottom edge of the strip, in a straight line along the edge following the point. From the same point, glue ribbon down the adjacent slope to the bottom edge. Trim off the excess at the bottom. Repeat for each point on the strip to create a crisscross pattern.

3 While the glue is drying, flip the felt over and create a polka-dot pattern by dipping the cork into the paint and then stamping. Let the paint dry.

4 To complete the crown, glue the ends of the strip together. To wear the crown the other way, just turn it inside out.

T-SHIRT BAUBLES

Don't throw out your favorite shirt because of one little stain! This material can be worn in so many ways.

WHAT YOU'LL NEED

- Old, colorful T-shirts
- Scissors
- Tacky glue
- Beads with large holes
- Toothpick

Experiment and play! One T-shirt makes a lot of necklaces, so if you mess up, you have plenty more to work with!

1 To make a beaded necklace, cut T-shirts into strips as thin as possible, ¼ to ½ inch wide. The strips should be at least 2 inches long.

2 Glue the ends of each strand together, then slip on a bead to cover each joint. Use a toothpick to help thread the fabric strips through the bead holes. Add a dab of glue at each point so the bead stays in place. Repeat to reach the desired length, and then knot.

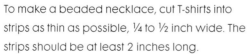

3 To make a tassel necklace, cut a 1-inch-wide-by-2-inch-tall piece of T-shirt and fringe it vertically (see the Fringing lesson on page 120). Roll it horizontally and glue the unfringed end into the hole of a bead. (Use the toothpick to help get the fabric into the bead.)

4 To finish the tassel necklace, glue the ends of two 10-inch-long T-shirt strips into the other hole of the bead. Knot in the back.

ARROW HEADS

You don't have to wait until February to get a visit from Cupid.

WHAT YOU'LL NEED

- Blue, magenta, white, and pink wool felt (available from MagicCabin.com)
- Scissors
- Hot-glue gun
- Thin thread

FOR THE HEADBAND
- 1 chopstick
- 1 headband

FOR THE BUN STICKS
- Two 5-inch wooden knitting needles

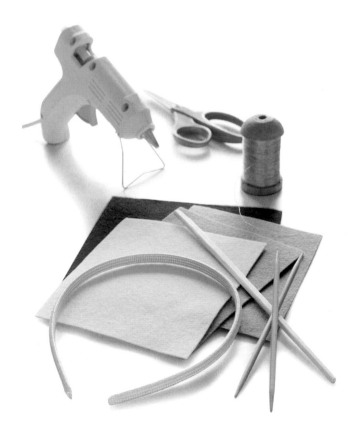

HEADBAND

1 For the arrowhead, cut three equilateral triangles from the blue felt, about 2 inches per side. For the tail feathers, cut one right triangle from each of the three remaining felt colors, with long sides of about 2 inches and short sides of ¾ inch.

2 Cut the chopstick into two equal halves.

3 Glue the blue equilateral triangles evenly around the tip of the pointed half of the chopstick, applying a line of glue down the center of each triangle. Make sure the top point of each triangle lines up with the point of the stick. Then glue the edges of the three triangles together to create a three-dimensional arrowhead.

4 Fringe each tail feather (see the Fringing lesson on page 120) along the hypotenuse. Leave at least ⅛ inch intact.

5 Apply a thin line of glue along the three long edges of the tail feathers, opposite the fringing, and glue them evenly around one end of the other half-chopstick.

6 While the glue is drying, further secure the tail feathers to the stick by tying a 3-inch piece of thread around them, making sure it goes between the fringe, and tying a knot. Trim the ends of the thread. (This process is similar to the traditional method of arrow making, called fletching.)

7 Glue the undecorated ends of the chopstick to either side of the headband, making sure they form a straight line across when worn.

BUN STICKS

1 For the arrowheads, cut six equilateral magenta triangles, about 1 inch per side. For the tail feathers, cut two right triangles from each of the three remaining felt colors, with long sides of about 1 inch and short sides of ½ inch.

2 Glue three magenta triangles to the points of each knitting needle as described in step 3 of the headband instructions.

3 Fringe all six tail feathers (see the Fringing lesson on page 120) along the hypotenuse. Leave at least ⅛ inch intact.

4 Apply a thin line of glue along the long edges of the tail feathers, opposite the fringing, and glue three of them evenly around the end of each knitting needle.

5 Secure the tail feathers to each bun stick as described in step 6 of the headband instructions.

A little geometry lesson goes a long way in this project. An equilateral triangle is one with three equal sides. A right triangle has one 90-degree angle, and the hypotenuse is the side that's opposite that angle. See—crafting can be fun *and* educational!

BOTTLE-CAP BADGES

Become a decorated crafter with these lovely bottle-cap medals.

- Drink-bottle caps
- Cotton balls
- Solid fabric
- Hot-glue gun
- Glitter glue (available at Michaels Stores)
- Grosgrain ribbon
- Scissors
- Pin backs
- Tacky glue

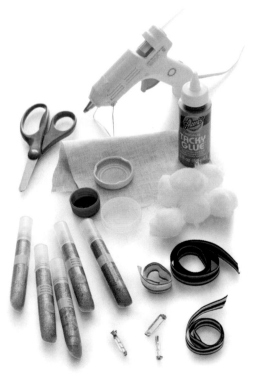

1 For each badge, glue cotton balls into the recessed part of a drink bottle cap. Glue three to four in a larger cap, and two to three in a smaller one.

2 Cut a circle of fabric large enough to wrap around the bottle top, lay the top in the center of the fabric, cotton-ball side down, and glue the fabric to the back (top) of the cap.

3 Decorate the front of the cap with glitter glue in any pattern.

4 Cut a 3- to 4-inch piece of ribbon, fold it in half to form an upside-down V, and glue the fold to the back of the cap. Glue a pin back just above the ribbon. Wear it proudly.

INSTANT SUPERHERO

If your hero finds himself without his cape, a dish towel, paper napkin, pillowcase, or handkerchief will suffice!

WHAT YOU'LL NEED

- 1 sponge
- Pencil
- Scissors
- Acrylic or fabric paint
- 1 dish towel
- 2 mitten clips
- Washi tape (available from HappyTape.com)
- 2 star stickers
- Clear nail polish
- ¾-inch-wide ribbon
- Two ¾-inch Velcro dots
- Needle and thread
- T-shirt

Remove the clips from the T-shirt before washing.

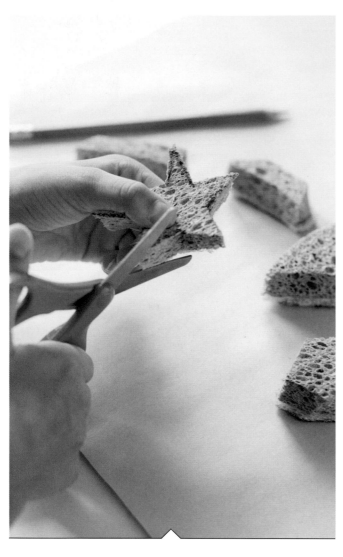

1

To create a stamp, draw a 3-by-3-inch star on the sponge and cut it out. (Or choose any shape you prefer.)

2

Dip the sponge stamp into the paint and create a pattern on the dish towel. Let it dry.

3 To make the cape clips, cover the tops of the mitten clips with washi tape, wrapping it around to create a clean edge. Put a star sticker on top of each clip, and coat with clear nail polish to seal it. Let it dry.

4 Thread a 1- to 2-inch piece of ribbon through the loop of the mitten clip, overlap the ribbon by at least ½ inch, and sew a piece of Velcro to the back (be sure to sew through both layers of ribbon, to keep it together). Sew the opposite side of the Velcro to the shoulder of a T-shirt. Repeat for the second clip. Clip the homemade cape to the T-shirt.

Turn the page for three projects using fabric dyeing!

It's taken many years to make dyeing fabrics an easy, mechanized task. One of the earliest known fabric dyes was a purple made from the petrified shells of a snail. Only kings and queens could afford robes in this color because it was almost as expensive as gold. It required so many shells that the snails nearly went extinct.

Now there are many different ways to dye fabrics, and a lot of them are safe and easy to do at home with your kids. Fabrics made from natural materials like wool or cotton will take and hold color much better than synthetic ones like nylon or polyester.

WHAT YOU'LL NEED

- 100-percent white wool felt (available from MagicCabin.com)
- Glass bowls
- Food coloring
- Water
- Clothespins
- Scissors
- Cotton swabs
- Cookie sheet lined with wax paper

1 Prepare a dye bath by mixing about 20 drops of food coloring into a glass bowl filled with ½ cup of water. The more concentrated the dye bath, the more vibrant your result.

2 For small pieces of felt, you should first try the dip-dye technique. If you want the color to bleed quickly up the fabric, wet it first, wringing out all excess water. For a subtler, more defined line, leave the felt dry.

3 Clip a clothespin to the corner of a piece of felt so it can rest in the dye bath. Submerge for 1 minute. With dry felt, you may have to submerge it longer. Check it, then resubmerge if you want a deeper hue.

4 For larger pieces of felt, dip a cotton swab in dye and then use it like a paintbrush to add patterns to the wet or dry felt.

5 Lay the dyed pieces on the wax-paper-lined cookie sheet to dry.

FABRIC DYEING PROJECTS

1

BOWS TO DYE FOR

WHAT YOU'LL NEED

- Scissors
- Dyed felt
- Hot-glue gun
- 1 bobby pin or 1 bow tie clip

FOR THE BOBBY PIN:

1 Cut a 1-by-2-inch piece of dyed felt.

2 Pinch the center together and wrap a ¼-inch strip of dyed felt around it; hot-glue the loop in the back.

3 Slip the bobby pin through the loop and add a dot of hot glue to secure it in place.

FOR THE BOW TIE:

1 Cut a 2½-by-4-inch piece of dyed felt.

2 Pinch the center together and add a few dots of hot glue between the folds to hold it in place.

3 Wrap a ¾-inch-wide strip of felt around the center and hot-glue it in the back to form a loop.

4 Slip the bow-tie clip through the loop and add a dot of hot glue to secure.

2

FELT FORTUNE COOKIE

WHAT YOU'LL NEED

- **Dyed felt**
- **Scissors**
- **1 pipe cleaner**
- **Glue**

1 Cut a circle 4 inches in diameter from the dyed felt.

2 Cut the pipe cleaner so that it's 4 inches long and glue down the center of the back (undyed side) of the circle.

3 Bend the felt in half so that the pipe cleaner is inside the cookie.

4 Next, angle the ends of the pipe cleaner toward each other, bending the wire at its halfway point to form a fortune-cookie shape.

3

FANCY FAIRY WAND

WHAT YOU'LL NEED

- **Dyed felt**
- **Scissors**
- **1 or 2 cotton balls**
- **Tacky glue**
- **1 chopstick**

1 To make the puffy star topper, fold the piece of dyed felt in half and cut a 3- to 4-inch star out of it to make two identical stars.

2 Glue one or two cotton balls in the center of one star, and then lay the other star on top of it and apply glue along the edges. Leave a small hole between two of the points.

3 Cut a few ¼- to ½-inch strips of dyed felt, glue them to the top of the chopstick, and glue the stick into the hole between two points of the star.

THE GREAT OUTDOORS

Where crafting
comes naturally.

UPCYCLED BIRD FEEDER

It seems only fair to turn one of *our* snack containers into one for our backyard friends.

WHAT YOU'LL NEED

- 1 small nut can (about 3 inches in diameter)
- Scissors
- One 6-inch stick
- Tacky glue
- Outdoor green craft paint
- 1-inch foam brush
- Twine
- 2 wooden beads

1 First, empty the can: peel the foil cover halfway back and remove the nuts. Cut off the unattached foil, then cut a ¼-inch slit vertically in the center of the remaining foil and fold the edges down on both sides to create a wide V shape. (We want the birds to enjoy their meal without injury.)

2 To create the perch, punch a small hole near the bottom of the attached foil with the end of the stick and push the stick through. Before the stick hits the back of the can, apply glue to the bottom edge of the stick and let it rest standing up in the bottom, back edge of the can until dry.

3 Paint the outside of the can and let it dry. Add a second coat if necessary.

4 Cut a piece of twine that's 5 feet long, plus as much as you'd like to use to hang the feeder. Find the center point of your length of twine and place the bottom edge of the feeder on it. Wrap each end of the twine around the can about three times, until both ends are once again at the top. Tie a knot, thread the beads over the two ends of the twine, and hang your feeder outside for your feathered friends.

ROCK GARDEN

Who would think that mixing sticks and stones (with a little tissue paper) would create such a sweet flower garden?

WHAT YOU'LL NEED

- Tissue paper in various colors
- Scissors
- Smooth rocks
- Mod Podge
- 1-inch foam brush
- Thin sticks
- Green paint
- Paintbrush
- E-6000 glue
- Green raffia or ribbon
- Small D-rings

1 To make the flower petals, cut approximately ½-inch-tall petal shapes freehand, leaving the tissue paper in its original fold. Do a few of each color so you have a variety of shapes and sizes.

2 Using a foam brush, coat one side of a rock with a thin layer of Mod Podge and begin arranging petals on top of the Mod Podge while it's wet. Paint another layer of Mod Podge on top of the tissue paper. Let everything dry.

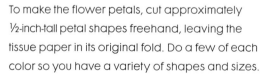

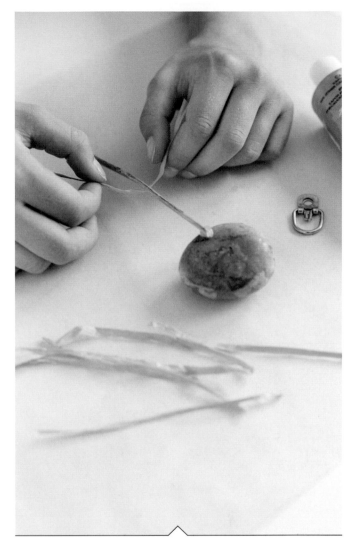

3 To make the stem, paint a thin stick green and let it dry. Attach it to the rock with E-6000 glue.

4 To give the flower leaves, tie a 4- to 5-inch piece of green ribbon or raffia to the stick. To hang, glue a small D-ring to the back of the rock with E-6000 glue. Let the glue dry completely before hanging. Repeat steps 1 through 4 for as many rocks as you'd like in your garden.

BEDAZZLED BRANCHES

This is a great project to use up the last drops of paint, ribbon scraps, and any other odds and ends in your craft bin.

WHAT YOU'LL NEED

- Sticks (mine were about 4 feet tall)
- Scissors
- Glue
- Various craft materials, such as:
  - Paint and paintbrushes
  - Sequins
  - Ribbon
  - Yarn
  - Colored tape
  - Glitter
- Pom-poms
- 1 tall vase or bucket

1 Collect sticks from your backyard, then decorate them with whatever craft scraps you can find. Alternate and layer materials—you can create a pattern with color or texture, or you can just paint, wrap, and glitter the bark out of them.

2 Glue pom-poms onto the sticks every few inches.

3 Display the sticks in the vase or bucket.

THE MUSHROOM AND THE SNAIL

Is this the name of a nursery rhyme? If not, I think it should be.

WHAT YOU'LL NEED

- Red, white, and blue felt
- Scissors
- Tacky glue
- Red embroidery thread
- Needle
- 3 to 5 cotton balls
- 1 wine-bottle cork
- 1 jam jar lid, 3 inches in diameter
- Moss
- Fishing line
- Pebbles (optional)

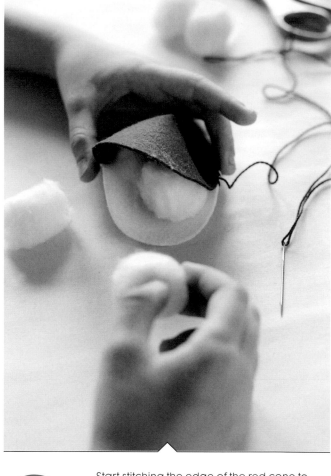

1

To make the mushroom cap, cut a 3½-inch-diameter circle from red felt and a 3-inch-diameter circle from white felt. Pinch the red felt so that the edge of the red circle overlaps about ½ inch on itself and glue in place. This will create a wide cone shape.

2

Start stitching the edge of the red cone to the white felt with embroidery thread. After you have sewn about half of the circle, stuff cotton balls between the red cone and the white felt circle. Continue stitching all the way around and knot the thread at the end.

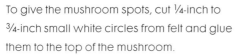

3 To give the mushroom spots, cut ¼-inch to ¾-inch small white circles from felt and glue them to the top of the mushroom.

4 Glue the cork to the underside of the mushroom, and glue the bottom of the cork to the underside of the jar lid, slightly off-center. Glue moss all over the lid so that it surrounds the mushroom stem.

5 To make the snail's shell, cut a blue and a red strip of felt, each about ¾ inch by 5 inches. Put one on top of the other. Roll them up and secure with glue. The inside felt strip will end up being a bit longer, so trim off the extra tail.

6 To make the snail's head, cut a single piece of red felt, ½ inch by 4 inches. Roll it up and secure it with glue.

7 To make the snail's base, cut another piece of red felt, ½ inch by 3 inches, fold each end to the middle, and glue. Glue the snail's head to the end of this piece, and the shell to the middle.

8 To give the snail antennae, cut a 2-inch piece of fishing line, fold it in half, and glue the folded point to the snail's head. Glue the snail on top of the moss, under the mushroom cap. Arrange pebbles around the lid and moss if desired.

WALNUT TOTEM

Walnut shells usually just get cracked and tossed—but why not put these beautiful casings on display?

WHAT YOU'LL NEED

- **Walnuts**
- **Paint pens**
- **Wooden beads**
- **Hot-glue gun**
- **Nutcracker**

1 Use paint pens to draw patterns on walnuts. Let them dry.

2 Hot-glue beads in between the walnuts, resting the top and bottom of the nut in the beads' holes. Be sure to glue these as vertically straight as possible to avoid tipping.

3 To make the base, crack a walnut by positioning the nutcracker perpendicular to the seam joining the two halves of the nut, and squeeze lightly along this line.

4 Once you separate the two halves, glue the totem to the top of one of the halves, with a bead in between.

THE FOUR SEASONS

Pinecones protect hundreds of seeds that grow into trees. But for this craft, the cones themselves become the forest.

WHAT YOU'LL NEED

- 4 pinecones
- Red, yellow, orange, and various shades of green yarn
- 4 dime coin rolls
- Scissors
- Tacky glue
- 2 to 3 pink straws
- 4 to 6 cotton swabs
- One ½-inch artificial bird (available from CreateForLess.com)
- White paint
- 1-inch foam brush

1
Using colors that correspond to spring, summer, and fall, wrap yarn in and out of the pinecones' scales until they look full. Leave the yarn attached to the skein as you wrap and cut it off only when you are finished. Glue the ends to secure. To create the trunks, cut coin rolls to about 1½ inches tall and glue them to the bottom of each cone.

2
To make the flowers for the spring tree, cut the straws into 1-inch segments. Snip four slits about ¼ inch long into the end of the straw, then flare out the five ends like petals. Cut a cotton swab off its stick and glue it into the center of the straw. Glue eight to twelve of these around the tree, wedging them between the scales.

3 For the summer tree, glue a small bird to the very top perch.

4 Since a winter tree has no leaves (or in this case, yarn), dab white paint on the tips of the pinecone as snow.

GARDEN-PARTY TERRARIUM

Create your own little world
(or in this case, party) in a jar.

WHAT YOU'LL NEED

- 1 glass container with a lid
- Pebbles
- Crushed charcoal
- Soil
- Small plants
- Chopsticks (optional)
- Patterned craft paper
- Scissors
- String
- Tacky glue
- Glue dots
- Plastic animals

1 Create the base for your plants by placing pebbles in your cleaned glass container. Then add a layer of crushed charcoal (one-fourth the depth of the pebbles), followed by soil (twice the depth of the charcoal).

2 Plant your greenery, beginning with the largest. If your container has a small opening, use chopsticks. Don't overplant—your garden needs room to grow.

3 To make the garland, fold a piece of craft paper in half and cut triangles on the crease about ½ to 1 inch long. Lay a string in the crease of the triangles and glue them together. To figure out how much string you need, measure across the terrarium and add about an inch to allow for swag. Attach the garland to the inside of the glass container by sandwiching each end of the string between the wall and a glue dot.

4 Cut 1-inch semicircles from craft paper and roll them into party hats. Trim if needed. Attach the hats to the animals' heads with a glue dot. Place your animals in and around the terrarium, and get your party started!

KING OF THE MOUNTAIN CROWN

This is the appropriate headpiece for His Majesty, Ruler of the Alps. (Or of the dirt mound in the backyard.)

WHAT YOU'LL NEED

- 1 topographical map
- Clear contact paper
- Scissors
- White felt
- Pencil
- Glue
- One ¾-by-20-inch piece of birch wood veneer

1 Laminate the map with clear contact paper and cut into a 6-by-10-inch strip. (If you don't have a map at your fingertips, you can download and print one from the Internet.)

2 Cut three 2½-inch-tall peaks from the center of the strip and make a diagonal cut from the bottom of the two outside peaks to the bottom corners of the strip.

3 To make the snow, trace the crown's three points onto white felt and cut out three triangles. Cut a zigzag shape on the bottom edge of the triangles and glue them to the tops of the crown's points.

4 Cut a strip of birch veneer that when attached at both ends rests snugly on your child's head.

5 Glue the veneer together, then glue the map to the inside of the veneer, opposite the seam. Now rule the mountain!

If you don't have white felt for the snow peaks, white paper or even paint will work just fine.

ART LESSON:
HOMEMADE CLAY

Turn the page for three projects using homemade clay!

Plates, mugs, floor tiles, planters, jewelry, bricks . . . the list of objects made from clay goes on and on. From early traces of hand-built water urns to the invention of the pottery wheel and the kiln (an oven that hardens the clay at a faster rate than air-drying), over the last 14,000 years clay has proved itself to be an art form we humans simply cannot live without.

As children get the feel of clay in their hands, it's best to start them off with basic lessons like rolling out slabs, making coils, or turning a lump of clay into a pinch pot, as these are the building blocks for many ceramic objects. Kids will get carried away, for sure. Stock up on the cornstarch.

WHAT YOU'LL NEED

- 1 cup cornstarch
- 2 cups baking soda
- 1½ cups cold water
- Saucepan
- Spoon
- Cloth

1 Put the ingredients in a saucepan and stir together over low heat until a dough is formed.

2 Cover the clay with a damp cloth and allow it to cool before using.

3 Store unused clay in a sealed container in the refrigerator.

HOMEMADE CLAY PROJECTS

1

COOKIE-CUTTER GARLAND

WHAT YOU'LL NEED

- Homemade clay
- Rolling pin
- Fondant cutter (small cookie cutter)
- Cooking oil
- Wax paper
- Toothpick
- Nail polish in a variety of colors
- String

1 Knead a baseball-size lump of clay to remove the air bubbles and then roll it out with a rolling pin until it's about ¼ inch thick.

2 Dip the sharp side of a fondant cutter in cooking oil, press it into the clay, then wiggle it around a bit to loosen it from the surrounding sides. Lift up the fondant cutter and gently push out the clay onto a wax-papered surface.

3 Use a toothpick to make a hole in the top of the charm. Repeat step 2 to make as many charms as you'd like. Let them dry overnight.

4 Decorate the charms with fun colored nail polish to give them an enamel-like glaze.

5 Cut a long length of string and create a fold about 1 foot from one end. Thread the bent string through the hole in one charm, fold the loop over the entire piece, and pull the charm and the rest of the cord through the loop. Repeat to complete your garland, spacing your charms 2 to 3 inches apart.

2

MADE-TO-FIT FINGER PUPPETS

WHAT YOU'LL NEED

- Homemade clay
- Paint markers or paint and a paintbrush

1 Break off walnut-sized pieces of clay and mold them around your fingers, pinching and smoothing until they have the look you are after. Carefully wiggle them off your fingers and lay them down to dry overnight (it might be best to insert markers into them to help keep their shape).

2 Use markers or paint to turn your creations into people or animals.

3

TOTE-ABLE TIC-TAC-TOE

WHAT YOU'LL NEED

- Homemade clay
- Toothpick
- Acrylic paint in two colors
- Paintbrushes
- Clear nail polish
- 8-by-10-inch drawstring fabric bag
- Colored tape, fabric markers, or paint

1 Roll the clay into ½-inch-thick coils.

2 Break off 3- to 5-inch pieces and curl them around to make Os. Smooth the ends together with a little water.

3 For the Xs, break off two 1- to 2-inch logs. Make a hash mark with a toothpick on the center of each log and add a dab of water. Press the hash-marked spots together, creating a seal. (This is called scoring.)

4 Let the Xs and Os dry, then paint them with acrylic paint.

5 Add a coat of clear nail polish on top to give them a little shine.

6 Make a tic-tac-toe board on the cloth bag with colored tape, fabric markers, or paint. Store the pieces in the bag.

ABSTRACT EXPRESSIONS

Projects that
encourage your
budding artist.

PEGBOARD PLAY

This is a two-part project: after an adult makes the board, the kid can design it. Over and over and over again.

WHAT YOU'LL NEED

- **Pegboard**
- **Bolts (size 10-24 by 1 inch)**
- **Nuts (size 10-24)**
- **Pot holder cotton loops (available at Michaels Stores)**

1 Insert a bolt into the back of the pegboard and tighten it to the board with a nut on the front.

2 Place a bolt in every other hole until you have the board covered to your liking.

3 Kids can make lines, shapes, letters, and pictures with the cotton loops.

Your pegboard can be any size. I cut mine down to 2 feet by 2 feet.

SYMMETRICAL STICKER ART

Use a penciled grid and simple dot stickers to teach kids the art of symmetry and pattern making.

WHAT YOU'LL NEED

- Stretched canvas or paper
- Ruler
- Pencil
- ½- to 1-inch permanent dot stickers (InStockLabels.com sells 36 colors!)
- Scissors
- Clear contact paper (optional)

1 Create a 1-inch-square grid by drawing intersecting horizontal and vertical lines 1 inch apart all down the canvas or paper using a ruler and a pencil.

2 Adhere dot stickers in symmetrical patterns by placing them in the grid and on its intersections.

3 Cut stickers in half or quarters to create different motifs.

4 Erase pencil lines. If you'd like, you can protect your art by covering the pattern with contact paper.

A fun way to teach a symmetry lesson is to apply stickers to one half of the canvas (either horizontally or vertically) and ask your child to count the squares and lines to mirror the image on the opposite side. Once they get the hang of it, they can design both sides.

COOTIE-CATCHER CRAFT

I remember making cootie catchers daily in the third grade. I can't believe it took me so long to see their stylish potential!

WHAT YOU'LL NEED

- 6 sheets of origami paper
- Tacky glue stick

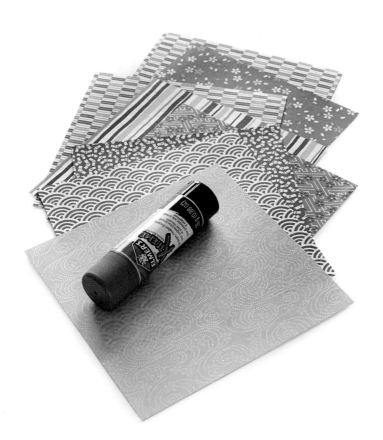

1 With the design faceup, fold the paper in half to make a rectangle, then unfold.

2 Fold it in half in the other direction to make another rectangle and unfold.

3 Fold two points together diagonally to form a triangle and unfold. Fold the other two points together and unfold.

4 With the design faceup, fold the four points into the center.

5 Keep folded, flip over, and fold those four points into the center.

6 Fold in half (with the points inside) to form a rectangle. Repeat in the opposite direction. Deepen the crease and unfold.

7 Push the four corners together and slip your thumbs and forefingers into the patterned compartments to complete the shape. Repeat steps 1 through 7 to make six of the same size.

8 Glue these six "cootie catchers" together on the bottom flaps to form origami orbs.

STRIPED PLATE ART

Let your kids design their own elegant wall decoration with disposable dishes and tape.

- 7-inch Bambu plates
  (available from Amazon.com)

- Mounting squares

- 3 to 4 rolls of ⅝-inch-wide glitter tape
  (available from AmericanCrafts.com)

- Scissors

1 Hang the plates close together on the wall in an abstract design using mounting squares.

2 Apply tape in long strips, crossing from one plate to another. Repeat in different directions, creating about five stripes.

3 Cut the tape that bridges the plates and fold the excess under.

RUBBER-BAND ART

You don't need a brush to paint like an abstract expressionist.

WHAT YOU'LL NEED

- Rubber bands
- Paper

FOR THE ROLLER

- 1 empty cardboard tape roll
- Paint or ink pad

FOR THE STAMPS

- Cardboard
- Tacky glue
- Ink pad

FOR THE PAINTBRUSH

- 1 pencil
- Paint

RUBBER-BAND STAMPS

1 Cut small rectangles of cardboard, a bit larger than the circumference of the rubber band that you're using.

2 Lay a rubber band down on a protected surface, apply glue to the top edge, and set a cardboard rectangle on top of it. Let dry.

3 Gently press the rubber band stamp onto the ink pad and stamp onto a piece of paper.

RUBBER-BAND ROLLER

1 Stretch five to eight rubber bands around the tape roll.

2 Roll the tape roll in a thin layer of paint or on an ink pad and then roll it onto a piece of paper to create multiple stripes.

RUBBER-BAND PAINTBRUSH

1 Gather six to eight rubber bands at the end of a pencil and wrap another rubber band around them to secure.

2 Dip the rubber bands into paint and use like a paintbrush.

Create the patchwork look shown here by first adhering painter's tape to the paper and peeling it off after the paint has dried.

PUFF-PAINT WINDOW CLINGS

Apply these clings to a window or frame. Then undo. Then redo. You get the picture.

WHAT YOU'LL NEED

- **1 loose-leaf plastic sleeve**
- **Dimensional paint in various colors**
- **1 float frame (optional)**

1 Draw shapes or pictures on the plastic sleeve with dimensional paint and let dry. You want the paint to be thick, about ⅛ inch. It's best to let it dry overnight, maybe longer in a humid climate.

2 Pull the shapes off of the plastic sleeve and stick them to the glass in your frame or in a window.

3 Move the shapes around to make new designs.

If you don't want to draw the decals freehand, you can print out shapes or pictures and slip them into the plastic sleeve for tracing.

SALAD-SPINNER ART

Ditch the lettuce and use your salad spinner to make some art. The best part? You never know what you're going to get!

WHAT YOU'LL NEED

- Cereal or cracker boxes
- Pencil
- Scissors
- Black tempera paint, plus 3 to 5 additional colors
- Paintbrush
- Tape
- Salad spinner
- Black cord
- Wooden beads

1 Cut 4-inch circles from recycled cereal or cracker boxes. Trace cups or bowls to get a perfect circle. Be sure not to exceed the diameter of your spinner basket.

2 Paint the blank side of each cardboard circle black. Let it dry. Fold a piece of tape and use it to attach the circle to the bottom of the spinner basket so it stays in place during spinning.

3 Squeeze healthy dollops of paint onto the circle, replace the salad spinner's top, and spin, spin, spin! If you are not satisfied with the result, add more paint and spin again. Remove the art and let it dry.

4 To make the hanger, tape an 8- to 10-inch piece of cord to the back of the spin art, thread on beads, tie a knot at the end of the cord, and hang.

Resources

BEADS, BELLS, AND JEWELRY-MAKING SUPPLIES AND TOOLS

BEAD CENTER
beadcenterny.com

If you travel to New York City to sightsee, go to the Statue of Liberty, to the Empire State Building, and then to Bead Center. Bring your rolling luggage; it's hard to resist their thousands of bead options!

TOHO SHOJI
tohoshoji-ny.com

Here you'll find a dizzying array of beads, cords, and jewelry-making supplies. But I go there mainly for their lovely selection of minibells.

DECORATIVE TAPE

HAPPYTAPE
happytape.com

This is the most appropriately named Web site ever. You'll indeed be happy you found it.

FABRIC

B & J FABRICS
bandjfabrics.com

From Liberty of London prints to awesome oilcloth patterns, this store has the best high/low range of fabrics you'll ever see.

THE CITY QUILTER
cityquilter.com

I discovered this store accidentally, and I'm so glad I did. It carries hundreds of affordable cotton fabrics that aren't too precious for kids to experiment with.

THE FABRIC EXCHANGE
thefabricexchange.com

From faux fur to clear plastic vinyl, if you know what you're looking for, this site has it. And it's all just a point and a click away.

MAGIC CABIN
magiccabin.com

With fifty-six colors of 100-percent wool felt, this is my go-to spot for one of my favorite materials.

TADAA! STUDIO
TaDaaStudio.com

With felt in almost 100 colors and felt beads in almost forty, you may want to ditch every other craft supply you own to make room for these.

GARDEN SUPPLIES

JAMALI FLORAL AND GARDEN SUPPLIES
jamaligarden.com

If you're in need of sheet moss, seashells, or a fabulous array of colored wire, you have no choice but to shop here. They sell garden supplies you didn't even know existed.

GENERAL CRAFTS

AMERICAN CRAFTS
americancrafts.com

Fresh, clean, and modern, this brand nails it every season with their new products. With kid-friendly patterns and colors, its paper can't be beat. They also sell amazing stickers, fabulous pens, and over twenty colors of brads in three different sizes.

CREATE FOR LESS
createforless.com

Point and click here to find your favorite everything, from unfinished wooden blocks to dimensional paint galore! There's a tab on the site dedicated to kids' crafts, so be sure to browse.

MICHAELS STORES
michaels.com

This store is like that best friend who never lets you down. From its amazing scrapbooking aisles to its endless selection of kids' craft items like pom-poms and pipe cleaners, you can always depend on Michaels.

PAPER SOURCE
paper-source.com

This is a great national chain and online source for a well-curated group of craft supplies, from washi tapes to rubber stamps to lovely sheets of handmade paper.

MISCELLANEOUS AND VINTAGE FINDS

ETSY
etsy.com

Etsy is best known for being a handmade marketplace, but it's now a great place to buy vintage and other unique craft goods like handspun wool, colored baker's twine, and felt beads. And that's just the icing on the cake. (And that reminds me, Etsy sells awesome party supplies too!)

EBAY
ebay.com

When I can't deal with pushing a stroller through the tight aisles of the local flea market, I shop for odd and vintage materials on eBay. It's always a gamble, but I've gotten good prices on vintage buttons, stationery, and ribbon. If you're willing to buy a lot that's a mixed bag, you can find some awesome deals.

PAPER

CARTE FINI FINE ITALIAN PAPERS
cartefini.myshopify.com

With over fifty colors of crepe paper, you will never need to shop anywhere again. Their paper is a heavier stock and feels more like fabric, making it harder to rip accidentally.

JAM PAPER & ENVELOPE
jampaper.com

You can shop for paper clips by color on this site. Enough said. (Oh, and it also has a massive inventory of envelopes, papers, gift bags, and gift wrap.)

PAPER PRESENTATION
paperpresentation.com

Headquartered in Manhattan, this is the DIY mecca for anything paper. I'm also addicted to their die-cut colorful tags and printer labels.

PARTY SUPPLIES

SHOP SWEET LULU
shopsweetlulu.com

If you want a well-curated party supply locale, Lulu is your lady! From striped paper straws to wooden demitasse spoons, you'll try your hardest to find a use for everything she sells.

ORIENTAL TRADING
orientaltrading.com

Management would have to kindly ask me to leave if this Web site were a brick-and-mortar store. From party favors to decorations to craft supplies, there seems to be no end to their playful and creative inventory.

RIBBON AND TRIM

M & J TRIMMING
mjtrim.com

Before you commit to purchasing anything, take at least three laps around this New York City store to see all of their ribbon, beaded trim, leather cord, lace—I could go on. And I didn't even mention their amazing selection of buttons and sequins.

TINSEL TRADING
tinseltrading.com

If they'd let me, I'd have my morning coffee brainstorm sessions on their floor. This store, full of ribbon, vintage beads, buttons, and baubles, not to mention holiday products, is so lovely and inspiring, you'll never want to leave. It tends toward the precious for kids' crafting materials, but if you're looking for that perfect handmade glitter or silver thread, indulge.

YARN

LION BRAND YARNS
lionbrand.com

Shop here for very affordable yarn that will look great whether as a pom-pom or wrapped around a glass jar.

PURL SOHO
purlsoho.com

Another dreamy store, it offers a gorgeous selection of yarns, threads, and fabrics too.

Acknowledgments

This book was a true labor of love, so it's time to share the love with everyone who labored with me, for me, and around me. To my editor and publisher, Lia Ronnen, who sat across from me at her desk and said, "I want to make the bible of kids' crafts with you," thank you times a thousand. To her associate editor, Bridget Heiking, who patiently combed over every step, every measurement, and every materials list, thanks for making sure t's were crossed, i's were dotted, and pom-poms were hyphenated. Michelle Ishay-Cohen, a huge thank-you for putting up with my fear of black and making my first book one that I am proud of. A very warm thank-you to Renata Di Biase, Sibylle Kazeroid, Nancy Murray, and everyone else on the Artisan team. And endless thanks to photographer Alexandra Grablewski, who stood with me through eleven shoot days to make it just right!

Thank you to Bridget Clegg, who put her flair and genius into this book. To Annie Nicholas, for devoting her nonexistent spare time to helping me prop and style the sets and kids. Thank you to SPM Communications, Michaels Stores, and CreateForLess.com for their generosity with the tools of my trade.

And to those who gave me a little push: Judy Goldberg, Amanda Kirk, Dan Schwartz, Ami Desai, Lindsay Senter, Aaron Stern, Jane Nussbaum, Micah Sommers, Scott Sternberg, Danny Seo, Bonnie Siegler, Gabrielle Blair, Jennifer Brett, Jack and Yvonne Cohen, Traci Gingold, and Dena Cohen.

I'm most grateful to Dana Points and the staff of *Parents* for letting me work out my craft skills on the pages of their esteemed magazine. And to the lovely and lovable Katie Brown, for the two-year boot-camp training. Thank you to Kathyann Gilbert for feeding, clothing, and entertaining my babies so that I could bury myself in buttons and beads. And to all of the gorgeous and patient children (and their parents) whose faces and hands brought these crafts to life: Oliver and Sommer Cohen, Hannah and Zachary Brett, Grey and Sidney Cohen, Sophia Kirk-Salazar, Finley Frenkel, Sophia Hall, Aden Jobarteh, Max Wolfe, Nicolas Verene, Natalie Glassie, Lilly Meyer, and Jane Minus.

Thank you to my overwhelmingly generous parents, Barbara and Dan Kingloff, who always said, "Yes, you can." And finally, thank you to my husband, Michael Cohen, who should really have a byline on the cover of this book. This man is beyond my partner in marriage and parenthood, he's my partner in late-night crafting, punny headline writing, and spontaneous brainstorm sessions. He never failed to give me his honest (read: blunt) opinion and to pat me on the back when I needed affirmation. As co-creator of my two best projects, Oliver and Sommer, he's so hired. Permanently.

Project Index